Barry Fan

Royal Chinese Horoscopes

Barry Fantoni's

Royal Chinese Horoscopes

The British Royal Family and their Chinese Animal Signs

First published 1988

To the memory of my dear father,
whose gifts continue to enrich me

British Library Cataloguing in Publication Data

Fantoni, Barry, *1940-*
Barry Fantoni's royal Chinese horoscopes :
the British royal family in the light of
their Chinese horoscopes
1. Great Britain. Royal families.
Astrological aspects
I. Title
133.5′892972

ISBN 1-85336-019-8

*Equation is part of the Thorsons Publishing Group Limited, Wellingborough,
Northamptonshire, NN8 2RQ*

Printed in Great Britain by
Richard Clay Limited, Bungay, Suffolk

1   3   5   7   9   10   8   6   4   2

Contents

Acknowledgements

While writing this book I made the not-unexpected discovery that there are only a limited number of sayings by any member of the Royal Family that can be deemed truly authentic. Those that come into this category are as well known as any stand-up comic's night club patter, and historical monarchs hold no greater treasure-chest of genuine royal remarks, as time and repetition often alter them out of all recognition. In our age, the Queen does not give interviews and the Royal Family as a whole tend to be understandably secretive about their true feelings. Now and again something personal slips out and the media pounce on it. Usually, royal secrets are printed for nothing more than their sensation value. But for the student of Chinese Horoscopes, each royal utterance often provides a major insight into the way a royal thinks or feels. An off-the-cuff remark here, a well-rehearsed speech there, all add up and, when seen as a whole, establish a firm, clear-cut picture of the influencing animal.

Research has played a major part in the creation of this book, and I would like to express my deepest gratitude to all those who have helped me sift through the hundreds of books, newspaper articles, magazine features, etc., about the Royal Family, both past and present. In particular, I should like to thank Elizabeth Buchan, a Rat who took time off from writing her very involved first novel to give me unlimited help and invaluable historical guidance. My thanks also go to my mother who, in typical Rooster fashion, worked out each animal year to the year dot, to Jane Qvortrup, a Buffalo who took the burden of my daily chores on her capable shoulders, and last but not least, my Rooster wife for her continuing love and support.

The books that I used for most of my research are listed in the Bibliography. I am indebted to both their authors and publishers, without whom this book would still be in its planning stage.

Introduction

As our most cherished institution, the monarchy maintains a central position in the hearts of millions. That the Windsor family is the most popular in the world is indisputable, a fact borne out by the cheering hundreds of thousands who greet them on visits, from Tulsa to Tokyo. Scarcely a day passes without a TV bulletin or newspaper headline about the latest royal exploit. From Fergie's new flying outfit to Charles's views on modern architecture the media seem spellbound, and rightly so. The Queen and her fast-growing family have an eternal fascination for a large number of people, and not only for those in Britain. The British Royal Family are truly international stars.

Because the British monarchy is the most popular in the world it has also become the most secretive. Understandably, they have built an almost impenetrable wall around their private lives to protect themselves from the ever-present gaze of press and public. Not surprisingly, this had led to much speculation about life behind the Royal Barrier. Of the millions of words written each year in the books and profiles which try to penetrate deeper into Charles, Diana, Anne, and the other members of the Royal Family, most are only guesses. But the Chinese Horoscopes change all this. No other system has the knack of getting beneath the surface and highlighting what really goes on when the shutters are up. With no more information than the year of birth, the Chinese Horoscopes can put the Royal Family under a unique kind of microscope. As we shall read, this ancient system gives us an insight into their inner characters that even their Royal Highnesses might find alarming.

We shall discover in this book, as the mystery of the Chinese Horoscopes unfolds and we examine the present Royal Family in terms of their animal signs and influences, that much of what this ancient Chinese science has to offer is astonishingly accurate— sometimes quite chillingly so. What's more, although the Chinese Horoscopes do not, and cannot, *predict* the future, they do have a simple-to-understand system that goes a long way towards it. By examining our individual animal sign in relation to the animal sign of a particular year it is possible to form a basic but effective guide as to what the future may hold.

Today, Her Majesty Queen Elizabeth and her family have not only arrived at a stable and unprecedented level of popularity, one which can easily be taken for granted, they also exercise a positive force for good in society. True, the time hasn't yet come when the British monarch catches a bus to the Palace as they do in Denmark or Holland, but the Queen's children are infinitely more accessible than were their predecessors. As we examine the Royal Family in terms of their animal signs we'll discover how the influence of the Rat, Horse, Tiger, Pig, and Buffalo, has helped to create this new-look monarchy.

The current upsurge of royal interest is largely a direct result of the influencing animal of the Queen herself. Born in the Year of the Tiger, Her Majesty's sign is fundamental to this present state of affairs. Being a figurehead is usually enough, but not for a monarch like the present Queen. As one who takes such an active role, she has reaped the rewards of a massive increase in popularity. And there seems to be no stopping the bandwagon of enthusiasm for British royalty. From the coronation of Queen Elizabeth in Westminster Abbey in 1953 (the Year of the Snake), to the wedding of the Duke and Duchess of York in 1986 (the Year of the Tiger), viewing figures for royal events have doubled and doubled again. The TV-viewing audiences around the world are now numbered in hundreds of millions and during the last three decades they have been privileged to witness all but the sacred moments of the British monarchy's major events.

As well as the coverage on TV and in magazines, the Royal Family are the subjects of hundreds of books. These come in all shapes and sizes, with the most serious authors trying to get beneath the royal facade and doing their best to determine what makes a royal person tick. It is clear that Anne (Tiger) is a bit of a loner, why? Edward (Dragon) as he steps more and more into the limelight displays a very short fuse. Will it grow longer with experience? And the rumours that Charles's and Di's marriage is on the rocks is now routine copy for some gossip writers. But the *real* Charles and Di seldom emerge. Conclusions about their lives, and indeed about the lives of all members of the Royal Family, behind the public image tend to be always less than satisfying. As I will show later in this book, and in great detail, Charles is a Rat and Diana is a Buffalo. This is *not* an auspicious relationship, and the Chinese would say it is one to be avoided.

The great step forward in public awareness that the Royal Family was entering a new phase in popularity came in 1973, with the wedding of Princess Anne to Mark Phillips. A massive 700 million watched the ceremony on TV, providing a quantum leap in public curiosity. For the first time the media as a whole, but the press in particular, felt free to speculate on the future happiness of Anne and her husband. Their potential togetherness was up for examination and no pundit was left out from giving his or her verdict. In 1986, Prince Andrew married Sarah Ferguson and the level of almost indecent speculation about this couple's life together went through the roof. I, along with astrologers, clair-voyants, and people who read tea-leaves, was asked for my opinion on how Fergie and Andy would fare along life's bumpy road. As I have said already, Chinese Horoscopes do not predict the future as such and so my contribution tended to rest on the fact that the Duke and Duchess of York are Rat and Pig respectively. This means that in the Chinese Horoscope chart for compatibility they get four out of five stars. A Pig and Rat partnership creates a strong platform for a lasting and light-hearted relationship, which seems amply borne out by the royal couple whenever they make a public appearance. Of all the pre-wedding pronouncements that have been proved false, most were made by Western astrologers. The majority said that, judging from their zodiac signs, Andrew and Fergie were not compatible. Clearly this is not the case.

The main reason why astrologers so frequently come unstuck in their predictions is that they only use the Sun and stars as a basis for their science. The Chinese Horoscopes, on the other hand, have the advantage of being centred on the 12 annual phases of the Moon. The Sun and stars have no direct influence over the Earth but the Moon is a very different matter. It has been known for thousands of years that the Moon influences both the tides and the behaviour of many people. Moonstruck, lunatic, looney, all these words come from a knowledge of the full-moon's influence. And even the female monthly cycle roughly coincides with the 28 days of a lunar month.

A question frequently asked is have the Chinese Horoscopes and Western astrology anything in common? The answer is a firm no. Attempts have been made by a few astrologers to link up the two systems, but they sit uncomfortably together. For years I had unsuccessfully tried to fit myself into the Pisces sign until in the end I gave up. But the moment I discovered I was a Dragon, everything became crystal clear. My whole life fell into shape. That was 14 years ago, since when I have more or less devoted my time to studying this ancient and wonderful science.

1
What are Chinese Horoscopes?

For the peoples of the East, their individual animal signs play an extremely important role in everyday life. Whereas in the West we treat our zodiac signs as little more than a form of entertainment, in the East the animal sign of one's birth is a serious matter. It is a system that pre-dates Christianity by five centuries and Western astrology by over a thousand years. Given its longevity, it's no wonder the present-day orientals pay so much attention to their ancient Chinese Horoscope and the 12 animal signs.

In China, everyone knows his or her sign and its particular influence. They also know how their sign relates to other signs, and are cautious when dealing with signs which are inauspicious. Although some animal signs go well together, such as the Rat and the Dragon, others are less compatible. It is not uncommon for a Chinese born in the Year of the Snake to avoid any dealing whatsoever with someone born in a Tiger year. Marriage between two such signs is virtually unheard of.

When understood, even at a very basic level, our animal signs can help explain why we do any number of things in a certain way. They highlight why some of us spend like there is no tomorrow, while others behave like a miser. Our influencing animals will determine the way we dress and the kind of work we do; how we spend our leisure time and who we find attractive. In China, the compatibility of animal signs is a way of life and governs friendships, marriages and business partnerships. An animal sign

13

is a means not only of discovering who we really are, deep down, but helps explain our true self to those about us.

It is not clear how the Chinese Horoscopes came into being but the legend, although obviously invented, like the story of Adam and Eve, does have a wonderful poetic charm which I find irresistible. The story begins at the time of the first new moon of the very first lunar cycle; the Buddha sent out invitations to all the animals in his kingdom to celebrate Chinese New Year. For reasons no one can explain, only 12 animals turned up. They were, in order of arrival; the charming Rat, the tenacious Buffalo, the courageous Tiger, the virtuous Cat, the lucky Dragon, the wise Snake, the independent Horse, the artistic Goat, the fanciful Monkey, the candid Rooster, the idealistic Dog, and, finally, the honest Pig. The legend has it that the Buddha was so pleased to see the 12 that he decided to grant a year in each of their favours. The animal in question would exercise his influence over all born during that year and their particular traits and characteristics would dominate it. Pigs, for example, would be honest and hard-working, Buffaloes would be single-minded and demand loyalty without necessarily repaying it.

Given this explanation, the obvious question, and the one I am most frequently asked is, 'If one animal has influence for a whole year, does that mean that everyone born in, say, the year of the Horse is the same?' This question, I must add, is usually asked with some degree of scepticism. I find that the best way to answer is by asking another question—is it true of *my* animal sign? Providing, of course, we have fully understood what our influencing animal sign means, the answer has to be yes. You could add that a thousand million Chinese can't be wrong! In 15 years I have never found one single example of a person who failed clearly to demonstrate a large number of their influencing animal's characteristics. And that is a fact. Having established that it is true of ourselves, the next step is to discover if those characteristics are also true of other people born in the same year? This way, we get a picture of real people and their influencing animals, rather than just having an abstract view of millions of people we have never met.

The golden rule in learning about the Chinese Horoscopes is to start with our own personal animal and its influences, then progress to our immediate family, and then on to friends. It was only when I had done this, and was completely satisfied that the system worked, that I decided to test the Chinese Horoscopes on personalities of the famous—men and women whose lives were well documented and easily accessible. In some cases, the famous names I selected were also friends or passing acquaintances— which was a big help. At this point I became fully convinced that the Chinese Horoscopes were accurate in every respect, providing us with an extraordinary system for discovering insights into ourselves and those around us.

With the aid of my Rooster wife, I listed 3,000 famous names and subjected them to the test. The results were staggering, and never more so than when dealing with members of royalty. More than any other social group, with the possible exception of film stars and pop singers, royalty is under constant scrutiny. And even if there is much hidden behind the tall walls that surround their stately dwellings, there is also much revealed. As I said in the Introduction, not a day passes without news of at least one member of the Royal Family hitting the headlines. With this book as a guide, the truth behind them will be made a lot clearer.

The Year of the Rat

1900 Jan 31 to Feb 18 1901
1912 Feb 18 to Feb 5 1913
1924 Feb 5 to Jan 23 1925
1936 Jan 24 to Feb 10 1937
1948 Feb 10 to Jan 28 1949
1960 Jan 28 to Feb 14 1961
1972 Jan 15 to Feb 2 1973
1984 Feb 2 to Feb 19 1985

Rats are born under the sign of charm and it is a great pity that their character is often coloured by the West's misconception of the rat's true nature. In the East, terms like 'rat race' and 'dirty rat' are unknown and rats are rightly considered to be creatures of great intelligence.

Rats are warm-hearted and their passionate personality is dominated by a sense of urgency. This means Rats are greedy for life, wanting to experience every moment to the full. Above all, the Rat is a supreme opportunist who lives for the moment and seldom plans for tomorrow. Few Rats have any concept of time. They are led by their highly developed senses, which have little or no regard for the hands of the clock. Rats are not farmers and Rat people seldom care much for possessions. If they have a full larder it doesn't often stay that way. Rats are not built for hard slog and when they make money it is usually as a result of their wits. As a general rule, Rats can deny themselves nothing.

Rats are quick-witted and have a sharp eye for detail, which provides them with a head start in business. In the story about the Buddha's New Year party and the 12 animals, legend has it that the Buffalo, being the most powerful, was the first to arrive but that the Rat pipped him to the post.

Waiting to the last minute, the opportunist Rat ran up the Buffalo's tail, over his back and down his nose, to become the first at the Buddha's door. It is said that the Buffalo has yet to forgive the Rat.

When plans go badly, or when they suffer a bad reversal, the normally outgoing Rat is the first to find fault. At times like these, Rats' sometimes shallow moral outlook will get the better of them and they will grumble endlessly. All Rats have an undercurrent of aggression, which frequently expresses itself in fretting about details and being over-concerned with trivialities. In extreme cases, Rats in distress may become obsessed with making plans and sticking to them at all costs. Their charm and easy-going manner is replaced by a tenacious stubbornness which nothing will overturn.

In their family life, Rats are devoted to their children, although the Rat parent tends to fret perhaps more than plan for their offsprings' well-being. The Rat home is usually comfy, rather than fashionable, with money going into the wine cellar as opposed to the three-piece suite. In work, Rats prefer flexi-time and avoid dull routine at all costs. Rats are ideal critics, capable of clear subjective judgement. Uncluttered by lofty principles, a Rat gets to the heart of the matter in a flash.

Those born under the sign of the Rat make uncritical friends whose advice is sound, well intentioned and always worth taking. In romance, a Rat is best suited to another Rat but should avoid both the capricious Goat and the candid Rooster. Although Rats and Buffaloes have a high compatibility in romance, when married their relationship deteriorates. Marriage favours a Dragon partner who, the Chinese say, is adored by the Rat. Dragons also make splendid business partners for the Rat.

The three phases of a Rat's life are marked by an easy childhood but a difficult middle period, in which romance and financial problems frequently abound. In the middle stage, the Chinese warn that a Rat might meet a sudden and violent end. However, with their senses less demanding, old age is kinder to the restless and rootless Rat. Even Rats with no more than an old-age pension are sure to find the bags of grain in the barn full, sweet and plentiful.

Famous non-Royal Rats

Shakespeare, Tolstoy, Mozart, Clark Gable, Marlon Brando, Wayne Sleep, Lulu, Andrew Lloyd Webber, Gene Kelly, Glenda Jackson, Enoch Powell, Gary Lineker.

The Year of the Buffalo

1901 Feb 19 to Feb 7 1902
1913 Feb 6 to Jan 25 1914
1925 Jan 24 to Feb 12 1926
1937 Feb 11 to Jan 30 1938
1949 Jan 29 to Feb 16 1950
1961 Feb 15 to Feb 4 1962
1973 Feb 3 to Jan 22 1974
1985 Feb 20 to Feb 8 1986

Buffaloes are born under the twin signs of equilibrium and endurance. On the whole, Buffaloes tend to be conservative in their thinking, shying away from the world of gimmicks and trend. Ruled by conviction, Buffaloes nevertheless suffer from a complex, and sometimes uncontrollable, heart. Unless Buffaloes can find expression for their deep-down feelings, they will direct their massive energy inwards. At this point the Buffalo personality may become extremely unpredictable and sometimes self-destructive.

To try to understand the inner workings of those born in the Year of the Buffalo is often a fruitless task. All attempts to get really close only force the Buffaloes to retreat even further into themselves. Admitting personal secrets, should they exist, is considered a sign of weakness.

Incapable of sharing power, Buffaloes are strong, resolute, and demand great loyalty from those around them. Returning loyalty, however, is quite a different matter. Buffaloes are born leaders and no one works harder to achieve a goal. With single-mindedness that is sometimes astonishing it is not surprising that few Buffaloes fall short of their objective.

Buffaloes are the essence of reliability. Even so, stubborn in the extreme, they are not given to self-criticism and have an incurable habit of blaming others for their own mistakes. Buffaloes are resolute and tireless in the pursuit of their ideals.

The Buffalo is essentially a masculine sign and female Buffaloes differ only very slightly. They love to garden and, given the chance, prefer to live in the countryside. Lady Buffaloes dress tidily and to suit themselves. But when they do decide to dress to impress, watch out. They dress to kill! A stable family life is crucial to both male and female Buffaloes and both tend to make authoritative parents.

At heart, Buffaloes are solitary creatures who prefer honest toil to bright lights and high society. They are one-offs who have done more than any other sign to alter the world in which we live. In romance, Buffaloes should avoid the Tiger at all costs. The Chinese are emphatic about this and say Buffaloes and Tigers are the worst possible partnership. Roosters and Pigs are compatible in romance, but only the Rooster provides the perfect marriage partner. Buffaloes are also attracted to Rats. Here, romance is OK, but *not* marriage. In business, a Horse may be a useful associate, but it must be remembered that Buffaloes do not share power. Bearing this in mind, it is not uncommon to find a Buffalo wife wearing the trousers. Because they have such complex hearts, few Buffaloes risk falling in love on a regular basis and casual affairs are rare. A Buffalo might find conquering the world a piece of cake, but conquering their heart is a non-starter.

The three phases of a Buffalo's life are quite distinct. The Buffalo child is often isolated. Finding it difficult to form close friendships, Buffalo children tend to rely on themselves for amusement. For example, a boy Buffalo might collect stamps while girls will read a great deal. Middle life is equally unsure. Here, marriages tend to go astray and work proves a problem.

Buffaloes might easily marry more than once and start a second family. The third phase will be easier, and in old age the Buffalo is discovered happily reliving the more memorable moments of a full life. But an unfulfilled Buffalo faces a less auspicious end. Here we find the Buffalo gone to seed; power exhausted and complex heart filled with bitter regret.

Famous non-Royal Buffaloes

Napoleon, Bach, Walt Disney, Charlie Chaplin, Twiggy, Mrs Thatcher, Boy George, Richard Burton, Peter Sellers, Jane Fonda, Alex Higgins, Fatima Whitbread.

The Year of the Tiger

1902 Feb 8 to Jan 28 1903
1914 Jan 26 to Feb 13 1915
1926 Feb 13 to Feb 1 1927
1938 Jan 31 to Feb 18 1939
1950 Feb 17 to Feb 5 1951
1962 Feb 5 to Jan 24 1963
1974 Jan 23 to Feb 10 1975
1986 Feb 9 to Jan 28 1987

Tigers are born under the sign of courage. Tigers are both brave and powerful, with a strong sense of their personal identity. For those born under the Tiger's influence to be *somebody* is paramount. But whatever and whoever the Tiger becomes, it must be of their own making, and Tigers will go to any lengths to prove themselves.

In some countries, Asia for example, the Tiger is a national symbol and is believed to act as a protection against the Three Great Disasters; fire, theft, and evil spirits. Tigers are great people for ideas and seem to possess a never-ending stream. They are not types to go unnoticed and the Tiger will frequently rise to a position of high command. Even so, Tigers seldom enjoy total responsibility and they prefer to be captains rather than generals. But whatever their rank, Tigers do not like being ignored.

Tigers will adapt easily to any role that gives them an opportunity to display their abundant courage and imagination. They have the ability to organise and inspire those under them, although it must be said that Tigers can sometimes be impatient with red tape. A low opinion of authority often finds the Tiger classed as a radical, and with good cause. Tigers are impetuous and born rebels. They love a good scrap and few are better equipped to win. It is a great mistake to tangle with a Tiger or to try to push one around.

For all their power and strength, Tigers have a serious flaw—they are short-paced creatures. First off the mark, a Tiger will quickly lead the field, but the chances of staying ahead over a long distance is remote. Stuck in the mud, the Tiger loses all sense of personal identity. Depression quickly sets in and it takes a massive effort to get the Tiger up and running. But once back in the race, a Tiger soon forgets about the tribulations of yesterday, concentrating all his or her great energy on the next exciting project.

Tigers are gregarious and extremely generous. In particular, when Tigers make new friends they tend to go over the top, giving everything all at once. In love, Tigers are truly reckless and will risk everything to obey their hearts. In fact, Tigers go through life taking risks, which is why the Chinese say that danger is a constant companion. Quick to praise, Tigers are also quick to criticize—which they do openly. Nevertheless, the Tiger, helped by a rich imagination, makes a first-class parent who teaches by example.

Because their emotions fizzle out, Tigers do not find lasting friendships easy and few other animal signs are totally compatible. The Tiger's natural partner, in every walk of life, is the idealistic Dog. They are both defenders of those less fortunate—the underdog—and combine well when faced with adversity. Tigers and Pigs are well suited, more so if the male is the Tiger. Like the Tiger, the Dragon is hot headed and marriage between these two signs is also highly recommended. Not advised is *any* partnership between two Tigers, as this is bound to fail. At all costs, the Tiger should avoid the Buffalo, a combination the Chinese say is certain to end in disaster.

The three phases of a Tiger's life will all be unpredictable, a word which could easily sum up the Tiger's character. During childhood, the Tiger will be a constant source of worry to his or her parents. Young Tigers bounce about full of vigour one second and go frighteningly silent the next. And Tiger girls are usually tomboys, who will always add a few lines to their parents' foreheads. The middle period, dotted with alternating self-doubt and over-confidence, is the most difficult. But once through the danger zone, a Tiger's old age is as peaceful as any Tiger is likely to want it to be.

Famous non-Royal Tigers

Beethoven, Nelson, Agatha Christie, David Attenborough, Richard Branson, David Steel, David Owen, Marilyn Monroe, Terry Wogan, Pamela Stevenson, Alan Coren.

The Year of the Cat

1903 Jan 29 to Feb 15 1904
1915 Feb 14 to Feb 2 1916
1927 Feb 2 to Jan 22 1928
1939 Feb 19 to Feb 7 1940
1951 Feb 6 to Feb 26 1952
1963 Jan 25 to Feb 12 1964
1975 Feb 11 to Jan 30 1976
1987 Jan 29 to Feb 16 1988

Cats are born under the sign of virtue, which in Chinese terms means that they inherit both social and artistic graces. Although an essentially feminine sign, males and females born in the Year of the Cat are highly refined and seem to possess an inner mystery. In some Eastern countries, the Cat is also known as the Rabbit or the Hare. But, regardless which of the names is chosen, the influence of all three is exactly the same. Cats are sensitive and circumspect in their day-to-day dealings and as creatures of habit they seldom act impulsively.

People born in a Cat year love beauty in all its forms and place a great emphasis on establishing a beautiful home. Cats have a fine nose for a bargain which often leads them to be collectors— usually of antiques and paintings. Cats dress elegantly, normally with an eye for high fashion, and lady Cats in particular are said to have wonderful hair.

Cats of both sexes respond poorly to pressure and emotional stress, and female felines have a tendency to cry easily. What's more, Cats may sometimes abuse their position if given power beyond their capability. In general, Cats do not worry too much about international disasters as they have an aversion to suffering. But should a Cat take on the world and its problems, the Chinese warn that he or she will quickly cave in. The Cat places home, comforts and family life above all else.

Because Cats listen well, their judgement, particularly on financial matters, is extremely sound. But since Cats do not deal easily with emotional upsets, their advice on such matters is usually less profound. However, Cats will always listen carefully when spoken to, and their readiness to sit quietly while others talk frequently casts them in the role of the diplomat—a job in which they excel.

Routine is paramount to a Cat's well-being and they are seldom found making sudden changes to their life-style. Methodical and cautious, the Cat's ordered approach to life has its uses. In business, when a Cat strikes a bargain, it will be for keeps. A deal is a deal. But if a Cat owes you money, they will pay you back to the very last penny. However, Cats might well find that their need for an ordered existence spills over into an obsession.

Cats are blessed with a quick wit and an often gossipy sense of humour. They adore good food and fine wines, and enjoy gossip even more. But there is something of the snob in every Cat which sometimes causes friendships to exist on a somewhat superficial level. Given a choice, a Cat will choose an evening in the company of fashionable people to one spent on their own. But the Chinese say that Cat ladies often prefer to live alone, keeping their secrets well protected.

Regardless of the charge that Cats (mostly toms) are randy devils, the Cat, as influenced by the Chinese animal sign, is frequently the reverse. A Cat person is usually devoted to only one partner, although it must be underlined a highly sensuous nature may sometimes overrule carefully cultivated fidelity. In marriage, Cats have splendid relations with practically all other signs, Dragon, Cat, Snake and Horse being the most desirable. The only two signs likely to cause problems are the high-handed Rooster, and, the Cat's favourite lunch, the Rat.

The three phases of the Cat's life are not distinct. All are marked by the Cat's love of beautiful objects, a well-ordered, though sometimes fastidious, routine and preference for agreeable and informed conversation. But there is a bonus in the shape of the third stage. In the West, Cats are thought to have nine lives, while the Chinese believe the Cat is blessed with longevity. Same thing.

Famous non-Royal Cats

Frank Sinatra, James Galway, Selina Scott, David Frost, Albert Einstein, John Cleese, Cary Grant, Ingrid Bergman, Bob Geldof, Evelyn Waugh, Griff Rhys-Jones.

The Year of the Dragon

1904 Feb 16 to Feb 3 1905
1916 Feb 3 to Jan 22 1917
1928 Jan 23 to Feb 9 1929
1940 Feb 8 to Jan 26 1941
1952 Feb 27 to Feb 13 1953
1964 Feb 13 to Feb 1 1965
1976 Jan 31 to Feb 17 1977
1988 Feb 17 to Feb 5 1989

Dragons are born under the sign of luck and there is no doubt that those born in the Dragon year are unusually blessed. In the West, the legend of St George has done much to damage our under-standing of the Dragon's personality, which is usually regarded as evil. However, in China the Dragon is the national emblem and considered the harbinger of the Four Great Blessings; long life, virtue, harmony, and wealth. Created from fable, the Dragon leads the famous Chinese New Year carnival, which provides a perfect clue to the Dragon's larger-than-life personality.

Dragons are usually showmen, characters who are both arro-gant and precocious. They are hot heads who let their hearts rule their heads, but at the same time few other signs are capable of such generosity. Dragon people love to stimulate those around them. This they do by virtue of their extraordinary self-belief; the more they believe in themselves, the more they pass it on to others. Put another way, the Carnival King is a mixture of cheer-leader and magician, which explains much of the Dragon's influence.

An important ingredient in Dragons' make-up is their desire for perfection. Once they set their minds on a task, Dragons will see it through to the bitter end, regardless of any merit involved. As a result, they are double quick to find fault with anyone who doesn't give 101 per cent, 25 hours a day, 8 days a week. Curiously, a Dragon is most critical of those he or she loves most dear. Prepared to forgive terrible wrongs, a Dragon will create an embarrassing scene over the silliest trivial incident. And no one holds a grudge longer. It goes without saying that Dragons are the world's worst diplomats and even poorer gossips—always getting their facts wrong.

For all their abundant wealth of self-belief and inner certainty, Dragons cannot stand routine of any kind. Should Dragons feel imprisoned—either spiritually or physically—they will almost certainly go mad. Once in decline, a Dragon tends to become lazy, fat, and bitter. But the Dragon who comes back will almost certainly reach the top, and stay there.

Impetuous and arrogant, Dragons give their time and money freely to anyone who asks. They are easily infatuated and chase endlessly after lost causes. Consequently, Dragons are often found making fools of themselves. But for all their outward brashness and apparent lack of sensitivity, the Dragon has a romantic heart that's as big as a mountain.

Because the Dragon is a deeply masculine sign, women born under its influence do not find life quite the same bowl of cherries as their male counterparts. Relationships are more difficult for female Dragons, who tend to want to run the whole works and accept little or no advice. Male Dragons, on the other hand, step into relationships with the ease of a duck taking to water. Only the Dog poses a real threat in marriage, where it is believed the Dragon's relentless self confidence only serves to underline the Dog's inherent anxiety. But the credit side of a Dragon in love is extremely high; Rat, Rooster, Tiger, Horse, Cat, and Snake all providing excellent partners. But Dragons, it must be added, do not make natural parents or nurses.

The three phases of a Dragon's life will be varied, marked by a difficult childhood. Here the baby Dragon will be misunderstood by parents and classmates. In the middle phase, the Dragon is expected to make as many friends as enemies. But fame and wealth will come easily. In old age, a Dragon will find a life without regret. Always ready to lead one more carnival, Dragons are very much what we make them.

Famous non-Royal Dragons

Jeffrey Archer, Salvador Dali, Bing Crosby, Geoff Boycott, Martin Luther King, Shirley Temple, Yehudi Menuhin, Zandra Rhodes, Roald Dahl, Mel Smith, Harold Wilson, John Lennon, Cliff Richard, Bonnie Langford.

The Year of the Snake

1905 Feb 4 to Jan 24 1906
1917 Jan 23 to Feb 10 1918
1929 Feb 10 to Jan 29 1930
1941 Jan 27 to Feb 14 1942
1953 Feb 14 to Feb 2 1954
1965 Feb 2 to Jan 20 1966
1977 Feb 18 to Feb 6 1978
1989 Feb 6 to Jan 26 1990

Snakes are born under the sign of wisdom. Unlike here in the West, where they are thought of as evil, in the East snakes are highly regarded. To be called a snake in China is a rare compliment, and the term is applied only in the case of someone acting with great insight or artistic skill. Snakes are also thought to bring good fortune in matters of love. The Chinese believe that a Snake in the family will help the rice grow fat.

Snakes, above all others, are guided by their intuition. They rely, more than any other sign, on their inner senses, which they use to help perform even in life's most simple acts. This is perhaps why the Snake is thought to have clairvoyant powers and the ability to bewitch. Snakes think extremely deeply, pondering long over a plan before putting it into operation. But their thought is not just a case of logical progression. Snakes 'think' with their spirit, which is why so many excel in the fields of painting, sculpture, and, above all, music. Snakes are also blessed with a highly refined sense of humour, which like art depends so much on intuition in order to be successful. Furthermore, Snakes have a pronounced spiritual awareness which frequently expresses itself by an interest in the religious life.

As well as being given to great insights, Snakes also suffer from long periods of inactivity. The word for 'lazy' in Chinese is the same as 'inactive', and it must be emphasized that all Snakes will undergo long periods in which they appear to be doing nothing. Do not be mistaken. It is at their most 'inactive' that Snakes are at their most productive. This usually takes place before the major changes which occur regularly in a Snake's life. In spite of periods of hibernation-like calm, Snakes have active minds. But do not ask Snakes to make up their minds in a hurry. Unless their intuition is running on all cylinders, Snakes will invariably make the wrong decision. As a result, the Snake makes a poor gambler. But once Snakes have set their minds on something, whether it be a new sexual partner or a new pair of shoes, nothing will stand in their way. Snakes are extremely possessive, especially in human relationships, and cling passionately to those they love.

The Snake sign is extremely feminine and, as a result, men who are born in the Snake year are seldom aggressive macho types. Snake men are often slightly reserved and well mannered, preferring to sit on the edge of a group to get its measure before joining in. Snake women, it is believed, love accessories and adore jewels. They hate violence and when faced with conflict rely on their power to bewitch to find a resolution.

Both Snake men and women are born with a powerful sensuality and it is thought that Snakes' influence will cause them to experience several sexual partners. The Dragon is a perfect lover for the Snake, as it is said that the Dragon loves the Snake. The Cat is another sign which gets high marks for compatibility, as does the Pig. But the Snake should beware of the Tiger—a total non-starter.

The three phases of a Snake's life are marked by what the orientals call karma—a state whereby each action subtly and inescapably influences the next. For the young Snake, life will be solitary and for the most part misunderstood. They grow painfully slowly, which will alienate all but the most dutiful parent. The Chinese say that Snakes in mid life often lose someone close. The Snake's almost mystical heart will provide plenty of tricky moments but there is comfort for the Snake in old age. The Chinese say that Snakes born in summer will find lasting happiness, but those born during a winter storm will always be in danger. For the Snake who survives there is often great material wealth at the end of the road.

Famous non-Royal Snakes

Abraham Lincoln, Mahatma Gandhi, Jackie Kennedy, John F. Kennedy, Christian Dior, André Previn, Picasso, Schubert, Victoria Wood, Liberace, Stefan Edberg.

The Year of the Horse

1906* Jan 25 to Feb 12 1907
1918 Feb 11 to Jan 31 1919
1930 Jan 30 to Feb 16 1931
1942 Feb 15 to Feb 4 1943
1954 Feb 3 to Jan 23 1955
1966* Jan 21 to Feb 8 1967
1978 Feb 7 to Jan 27 1979
1990 Jan 27 to Feb 14 1991

Horses are born under the twin signs of elegance and ardour. All Horses share two central characteristics, those of practicality and independence. But because Horses come in so many shapes and sizes, these traits frequently express themselves through many different channels. After all, a Shetland pony is not asked to perform the same tasks as a highly strung show jumper. As a result, Horses will be found doing any number of jobs, which they will perform with the emphasis on hard work and efficiency.

A strongly masculine sign, Horses of both sexes have an easy-going personality which they exploit to good advantage. Horse women tend to be witty and sociable, and what they just might lack in looks will always be made up for twice over by sheer style. Horses, remember, have elegance as one of their twin signs.

* The Year of the Fire Horse

Male Horses, with their natural sense of ease when addressing large groups and their great inner reserves, usually mirror the female Horse with their wit and clear heads. Horses think quickly, logically and seldom, if ever, cave in under pressure.

Another of the Horse's attributes is a great ability to work all hours and for any length of time. Few other signs can put their noses to the grindstone without flagging. And a Horse will never quote you a wrong statistic or give you a woolly-minded opinion. For all their high spirits, wit, and elegance a Horse deals in facts not opinions. And given a chance to lead, the Horse will jump at it.

As with all signs who gravitate to leadership, Horses do not like to be pushed around or ignored. Although slow to anger, the Chinese Horoscopes point out that once a Horse is seen in a rage the experience is never forgotten. And woe betide you if you are the object of this anger.

Horses also easily become bored, and not only with people. A Horse quickly changes jobs and hobbies and generally tends not to plan long term. They might *think* they have found a job or partner for life, but in reality it will be just another passing phase. However, once 'settled' in a family, the Horse will automatically become the key figure. But even then, they will probably invest more time in their work than in their children.

As a rule, Horses are not possessive or jealous about those they love. They require freedom above all else, and usually acknowledge that their partners might require the same. But Horses fall in love easily, and although they seldom get bitter or twisted should it not work out they do become extremely weak once smitten. Love is not logical and the practical-minded Horse never learns this simple fact. They think each new romance is the Big One, forgetting they have thought this a hundred times before. Cats and Goats provide stable marriage partners while Rats, Buffaloes and Monkeys draw the short straw. Two Horses are splendid in love, but the temptation to marry should be avoided at all costs. The risk of failure is too great.

The three phases of a Horse's life will be determined by the need for freedom. Young Horses tend to leave the stable early and the middle years will see many changes. It is also said that a Horse born in the summer has an easier life than those born in the winter. However, old age is kinder to all Horses, with their need to be independent at all costs finding a more flexible level of expression.

A word about the Fire Horse. Occurring every 60 years, the Year of the Fire Horse has a powerful effect on all those born under its sign. The Chinese believe that Fire Horses either have great good fortune or suffer sheer bad luck; sometimes they are dished out helpings of both. In short, nothing in a Fire Horse's life will ever be moderate.

Famous non-Royal Horses

Clint Eastwood, Paul McCartney, Chrissie Evert, Billy Graham, Chopin, Neil Kinnock, James Dean, Samantha Fox and Zola Budd (both 1966 Fire Horses), Rembrandt (1606 Fire Horse).

The Year of the Goat

1907 Feb 13 to Feb 1 1908
1919 Feb 1 to Feb 19 1920
1931 Feb 17 to Feb 5 1932
1943 Feb 5 to Jan 24 1944
1955 Jan 24 to Feb 11 1956
1967 Feb 9 to Jan 29 1968
1979 Jan 28 to Feb 15 1980
1991 Feb 15 to Feb 3 1992

Goats are born under the sign of art and are thought to be the most uniquely feminine of all the 12 signs. Appreciated for their shy and gentle manners, Goats are acclaimed above all as the Bringers of Peace. They are quick to react against conflict and only ever strike a militant pose in an attempt to restore harmony. However, it must be added that the Goat's love of a peaceful world is not based on some glorious universal ideal; quite the reverse is true. The Goat's code is quite simply that a harmonious world provides the socially pleasurable opportunities for which all Goats crave. The Japanese have an expression which sums up the Goat personality beautifully—*I-Shoku-Ju*, which roughly translated means a love of the senses; food, clothes, and comfort.

Because of their sign, art, Goats make the most wonderful performers. In fact, it is impossible to stop a Goat performing at any level. Whenever a Goat turns his or her considerable talent to

37

anything that is even vaguely demanding of a show, no matter whether it's *Hamlet* at the Old Vic or a *cordon bleu* supper, we are likely to witness a performance of Oscar-winning proportions. No one can dance or act as well as a Goat, and their great pleasure in performing provides an unexpected advantage in the party throwing stakes. Although the Goat faces tough competition for the title of top hostess, namely from the Horse and the Pig, she frequently runs out the winner.

The reason Goats enjoy such spectacular success socially has a lot to do with their constant need to be in the centre of the limelight. With the attention full on them Goats thrive, but it is here that they face the greatest danger. Goats need tethering to make the most of themselves and left to their own devices they are prone to wander—usually in search of the next good time. The Chinese describe Goats as capricious (which hits the nail on the head since the word 'capricious' comes from the Latin for Goat: *caper* or *capra*) they follow trends rather than create them. But once tethered, to a task or an ambition, a relationship or a dream, a Goat will invariably hit the jackpot.

Although they might make money, in business Goats tend to overstate their case or choose the wrong moment to do so. They should avoid working in sales, unless as part of a team. And should they take on supreme responsibility, Goats will do well to appoint less-fickle advisers. No stranger to hard work, Goats usually spend what they earn—most often on themselves. Goats are acquisitive and love buying beautiful objects, clothes, paintings, and all the trappings of the *dolce vita*. But they are also generous creatures, providing you are in their good books.

The Goat's waywardness frequently expresses itself in matters of the heart, where long-term relationships prove difficult. Nevertheless, Goats can hope to find understanding, love, and companionship with a number of other signs, notably the Horse, who rates five stars in all departments. In addition Cats, Pigs, and Monkeys all have high marks for compatibility.

The first of the three phases of life finds young Goats clinging to the family, and, as throughout their lives, they use tears and tantrums to get their own way. Breaking parental ties is tough for a Goat and it is noted that Goats invariably live close to the family home. Driven by their senses, Goats experience a number of emotional ups and down through the middle period, the heart always ruling the head. But Goats are quick to learn and seldom make the same mistake twice. Money, too will bring its share of problems. But in the last phase, when the Goats realize that their own patch is truly worth cultivating, there will be peace and abundance.

Famous non-Royal Goats

Lord Olivier, Mick Jagger, Ian Botham, Anna Ford, Margot Fonteyn, Sir Terence Conran, Dame Peggy Ashcroft, Boris Becker, Cecil Parkinson, Mikhail Gorbachev.

The Year of the Monkey

1908 Feb 2 to Jan 21 1909
1920 Feb 20 to Feb 7 1921
1932 Feb 6 to Jan 25 1933
1944 Jan 25 to Feb 12 1945
1956 Feb 12 to Jan 30 1957
1968 Jan 30 to Feb 16 1969
1980 Feb 16 to Feb 4 1981
1992 Feb 4 to Jan 22 1993

Monkeys are born under the sign of fantasy. Of the 12 signs, Monkeys are the closest to humans. They are endowed with all the very best that mankind offers and, unfortunately, many of his worst faults. On the credit side, Monkeys are blessed with great intelligence. They have a high regard for knowledge and are capable of thinking through even the most complex problems, seemingly without effort. Charming, resourceful, with a strong sense of their own value, Monkeys use a potent mixture of wit and wisdom to attain their goals—and there are usually dozens.

If the Monkey has one outstanding quality it is the power to adapt. Given any number of quickly changing circumstances the Monkey will move smoothly from one to another. Monkeys are nothing if they are not wheeler-dealers, and with a sharp eye they usually settle on the most profitable. Monkeys are not originators as a rule but they are brilliant at taking the ideas of others and skilfully adapting them to suit their own needs. A Monkey, it is said, will try anything once.

The last to admit it, Monkeys have a cool head and a powerful memory, which tends to give them a great advantage in business. Coupled with a pronounced acquisitiveness, the Monkey's business acumen invariably leads to a healthy bank balance, one which, the Chinese Horoscopes warn, is usually treated with a tight fist. However, few are more generous with help or praise. Highly organized, though sometimes prone to casting superficial judgements, Monkeys are gifted creatures with an extraordinary ability to make people believe whatever they say. The Chinese again warn against this, pointing out that since their sign is fantasy, Monkeys find it difficult to distinguish between fact and fiction.

Most Monkeys enjoy a highly sophisticated sense of humour. This they might easily use to get out of a tight corner, which are more common for a Monkey than any other sign. Intrepid travellers, Monkeys see an open road, both as a challenge and as a route to new experiences. Once Monkeys have decided on a course of action, they must act there and then. If not, they will quickly move on to something else. And when a project turns sour you won't find Monkeys nursing their wounds. Quick to recover, they will be up and running in no time at all.

Because they have a constant need to develop new interests, Monkeys frequently find that long-term relationships elude them. No one person ever truly satisfies a Monkey, the reason being that Monkeys are not seeking satisfaction. It is the love of new experiences that has the Monkey in its grip. One view of the romantic Monkey states that they prefer intrigue to love itself. However, a Monkey looking for a partner might well search out another Monkey, a relationship which scores high marks. Both Dragons and Pigs get maximum marks of the scale of compatibility, with perhaps the Dragon/Monkey pairing just in front (top in both business *and* pleasure). Although they handle most signs with ease, Monkeys should steer clear of Horses and Roosters. And Monkeys should remember the Dragon is the only sign to get one over them.

41

The first phase of a Monkey's life will be dictated by an unsettled childhood in which there will be continual brushes with authority. A lack of stability at home and a trail of failed relationships will dominate the second phase. But there will usually be enough money to pay the rent and alimony. Old age is kinder to the inquisitive Monkey, in spite of the fact that the Chinese say that Monkeys are in danger of meeting a sudden end in a far place.

Famous non-Royal Monkeys

Leonardo da Vinci, W. G. Grace, Liz Taylor, Sebastian Coe, Shirley Conran, Pope John Paul II, Tim Rice, Angela Rippon, Diana Ross, Stephen Hendry, Frank Bough.

The Year of the Rooster

1909 Jan 22 to Feb 9 1910
1921 Feb 8 to Jan 27 1922
1933 Jan 26 to Feb 13 1934
1945 Feb 13 to Feb 1 1946
1957 Jan 31 to Feb 17 1958
1969 Feb 17 to Feb 5 1970
1981 Feb 5 to Jan 24 1982
1993 Jan 23 to Feb 9 1994

Roosters are born under the sign of candour. The Chinese say that there are two basic Roosters; those born between 5 and 7 in the morning and between 5 and 7 in the evening, who are called sunup/sundown Roosters, and those born at any other time. The sunup/sundowners tend to be spendthrifts. For this Rooster, money is something to spend and having an overdraft is just something they learn to live with. The reverse side of the coin is the save-every-penny Rooster. These birds are the kind to spend all morning walking round the supermarket looking for the day's bargain. But even the hard-saving Rooster is tainted with the spendthrift influence, and once they have saved a tidy pile, it is frequently blown in a flash on something quite unexpected.

Conservative with a small 'c', and often with a big one, Roosters are no-nonsense folk. They are generally easy to spot in a crowd, being self-assured, talkative, and frank. Male Roosters are usually just plain boastful. No other sign is more outspoken or moral. Whereas some animals have an influence which produces a low moral horizon and few if any scruples, the high-minded Rooster has more than enough to go round. And it must be added that even the shy Rooster usually manages to get the limelight, perhaps for the very reason that they will be the one person spotted sitting alone in the corner of a crowded room. Getting attention is a natural function of the Rooster influence and the Chinese say that their sign has a military significance. Indeed, with all those wonderful feathers and red crown it is easy to see why.

All Roosters are exceptionally methodical. They adore keeping notebooks and are forever writing all manner of things on bits of paper, which are then filed and put away. They also tend to build castles in the air, which leads to another prominent feature of their personality; to promise more than they can deliver. A little short of initiative at times, Roosters are not scared of hard work. Once they find a task that fits their rigid temperament nothing will stand in Roosters' way.

For all their conceit and candour, Roosters are deeply secretive about their private relationships. They might boast about many things, but their sex life is not usually one of them. Although they may lack tact, there can be no doubting a Rooster's honesty and in a relationship it would be a very rare Rooster indeed who would be the first to wander. This is especially the case in female Roosters. Quick to point out the faults in others, Roosters of both sexes are not so happy about being criticized, or even teased, themselves.

Although naturally good mixers, Roosters might be just as contented with their own company. Left on their own, Roosters are not likely to fret and spend all day phoning up friends. However, female Roosters are more than happy to spend a night out with the girls. In terms of marriage, Roosters have three very strong masculine signs as perfect partners—which bodes better for female than for male Roosters. Buffaloes, Dragons and Horses all score high, if not maximum, points for compatibility. For male Roosters, a Snake offers another choice for a long-term relationship.

The first of a Rooster's three phases, childhood, is thought to be the most auspicious. Rooster children are bright and attentive and make the most of their youthful exuberance. Middle years are often dogged by money matters and their over-the-top morality tends to break up rather than heal marriage difficulties. Old age finds the Rooster, more often than not, a rather solitary creature. Happy in their gardens (which all Roosters love) they will at least have their dreams.

Famous non-Royal Roosters

Wagner, Steve Davis, Joan Collins, Yoko Ono, Ken Livingstone, Dirk Bogarde, Michael Caine, Nancy Reagan, Michael Heseltine, Hardy Amies, Mary Quant, Steffi Graff.

The Year of the Dog

1910 Feb 10 to Jan 29 1911
1922 Jan 28 to Feb 15 1923
1934 Feb 14 to Feb 3 1935
1946 Feb 2 to Jan 21 1947
1958 Feb 18 to Feb 7 1959
1970 Feb 6 to Jan 26 1971
1982 Jan 25 to Feb 12 1983
1994 Feb 10 to Jan 30 1995

Dogs are born under the sign of idealism and, no matter what size or shape they come in, a dog's honesty and loyalty are there for all to see. Whether a stray down on his luck or Cruft's champion of champions, the eternally touching expression in a dog's eyes is invariably one of unconditional devotion. And on the subject of diversity, few animal signs have such a wide range of influences as 'Man's Best Friend'. Although all Dogs are capable of great devotion, not all can be relied on to show it at first meeting. This aspect of the Dog's sometimes unpredictable character is succinctly and wittily summed up by the sixteenth-century vicar and natural historian the Rev. Edward Topsell. He wrote, 'There be some Dogs which bark and do not bite, Dogs which bark and bite, and some which bite bitterly before they bark'.

Champion of the underdog, Dog people will never sit on the sidelines. The Chinese see Dogs as men and women of the

Left—strong advocates for change and social reform. Indeed, most Dog people will seek out injustice and fight it with every means possible. Once a Dog has been given a task worthy of his or her trust, no other animal sign can equal their stubborn determination to see it through at all cost. Equality, freedom, and justice are what Dogs fight for, and they demand that their open, and sometimes blunt, voice is heard.

It is worth always remembering that once you have earned a Dog's trust—something that will seldom be given lightly—you may count on that person for anything. A Dog will move mountains to carry out a task, or prove their worth. But it must be stressed that for all their warmth and devotion, Dogs will not easily forget or forgive an act of cruelty. Mistreat a Dog and you will find yourself no longer the object of his or her devotion. In these cases, where Dogs have been badly abused, it is advisable to take great care when building up a relationship. And it may be the case that the Dog in question might never fully overcome their grievances. Dogs feel hurt very deeply and they have little or no technique for dealing with emotional pain.

Stubborn, watchful, and often defensive, Dogs are quick to criticize our lack of concern for the world's injustices, and fear of not being thought to do their best frequently causes Dogs to become anxious. A Dog will speak out of turn and appear cynical at times, often unaware of the efforts of those around to do their best. The Dog's main ambition is to please and to be thought well of. Failure to be thought well of can swiftly lead Dogs into a state of anxiety, which they find almost impossible to escape from. This in turn leads a Dog to respond to life's setbacks with more pessimism than is normally thought to be healthy. Faced with uncertainty or lack of purpose, Dogs will never fully distinguish the wood from the trees.

Although Dogs might easily make money, often huge sums, it will never bring the comforts or security it does for many others. In fact, Dogs care virtually nothing for wealth, and place their only high premium on personal relationships. But because of their ever-present habit of barking at strangers, Dogs find meeting the ideal partner a tough job. In marriage, only Tigers and Pigs offer five stars, while Horses also provide a lasting, four-stars relationship. Dogs, however, should avoid the Dragon and the Goat unless there is *real* understanding.

The three phases of a Dog's life will all be affected by the tendency to be anxious. Dog children will act dutifully and stay close to home and parents. The middle period often calls for flexibility, a quality that Dogs find difficult unless there is a true purpose to it. Old age offers no respite, adding a sad but true reflection on the old expression; it's a Dog's life. But it must also be stressed that Dog people are the most noble of all.

Famous non-Royal Dogs

Winston Churchill, Mother Teresa, Elvis Presley, Sylvester Stallone, Mary Whitehouse, Daley Thompson, Michael Jackson, Madonna, Brigitte Bardot, Edwina Currie.

The Year of the Pig

1911 Jan 30 to Feb 17 1912
1923 Feb 16 to Feb 4 1924
1935 Feb 4 to Jan 23 1936
1947 Jan 22 to Feb 9 1948
1959 Feb 8 to Jan 27 1960
1971 Jan 27 to Feb 14 1972
1983 Feb 13 to Feb 1 1984
1995 Jan 31 to Feb 18 1996

Pigs are born under the sign of honesty. Whereas the West tends to downgrade the pig's status, the East is far more enlightened. They consider it a compliment to be called a Pig, knowing the great value that comes from having a Pig in the family. A Chinese proverb says, 'A teacher should never abandon his books, or the poor man his pig'. And no wonder. No other animal works harder and plays harder. Well informed and gregarious, the hail and hearty Pig loves company and shines in a happy throng.

Although the Pig is essentially a masculine sign, both male and female Pigs have one characteristic in common—they really go to town when it comes to their wardrobe. Others may simply get dressed, Pigs dress up. Spot someone in a snazzy outfit, perhaps a little over the top, and odds are that you're looking at a Pig. Not generally career people, Pig ladies excel in a domestic environment. They are the best cooks of any of the 12 signs—generally cooking honest food, and lots of it. On the other hand, the Chinese point out that a small number of Pigs have homes a bit like . . . well, pigsties. These Pigs care nothing for their surroundings, are not very bright upstairs and dress in anything that comes to hand. But both Pig types live just the way they want, organizing life to suit themselves.

Pigs, male and female, tend to be big-hearted and well organized people who are not given to much self-analysis or bothered by world problems. They are down-to-earth and durable, which is why the Chinese say that Pigs seldom go hungry. Because of this, the Pig tends to be over-confident and is therefore a prime target for confidence tricksters of all sorts. Pigs, it is said, are easily duped in both romance and business. But once taken for a ride, the previously credulous Pig becomes over-suspicious and rapidly constructs an emotionally defensive wall, which is almost impossible to break down.

Pigs usually get straight to the point, having first waited in the background to gauge their position. Although they argue forcibly, Pigs are prone to getting their facts wrong. Pigs hate disputes of any kind and handle them badly; first making their point too strongly and then retreating when the going gets rough. However, Pigs do not bear grudges and because they hold themselves in such high self-esteem, care little of what others think. 'Take me as you find me' is the Pig's motto.

Pigs in love pose a problem for themselves and everyone else. They fall in love far too easily and tend to wear their hearts on their sleeves. No other sign has so many stars for auspicious relationships. The Chinese emphasize the point by saying that Pigs, lacking initiative, will always perform better in partnerships. In marriage, only three animal signs score less than 75% (the Dragon, the Buffalo and the Rooster) while Monkeys, Dogs and Pigs get the maximum. Pigs approach falling in love as they do everything else, with a robust but touching honesty.

The three phases of a Pig's life will not be greatly varied. The Piglet will enjoy a well-balanced childhood, although some dreams might not always be realised. Love poses a problem to a

Pig in midlife, as do the ever-present confidence tricksters, but the Pig's ability to work all hours will usually ensure there's enough in the bank to compensate for a broken heart. Old age holds no fears and the Pig who gets to his or her three score and ten will have a full and happy final stage, reflecting on the many busy hours.

Famous non-Royal Pigs

Ronald Reagan, Fred Astaire, Ginger Rogers, Woody Allen, Elton John, John McEnroe, Noel Coward, Brian Clough, Robin Day, Tracey Ullman, Sir Robin Day, Ben Elton.

2
The Prince and Princess of Wales

The Prince of Wales
Birthdate: 14 November 1948
Born in the Year of the Rat

A pop-music pundit once wrote, 'It is not easy being Paul McCartney'. I agree that it is difficult to imagine what life is like for the multi-millionaire ex-Beatle, but waiting to be King of the United Kingdom of Great Britain and Northern Ireland, and of other Realms and Territories, Head of the Commonwealth and Defender of the Faith certainly can't be any easier. What's more it looks as if Prince Charles's wait will be a long one. The reason why Prince Charles will not ascend to the throne in the foreseeable future has more than anything to do with his mother's influencing animal.

Her Majesty the Queen is a Tiger (born 1926) and is typical of her sign. She is healthy, vigorous, and, in keeping with Tigers everywhere, the Queen has an awesome sense of duty. This leaves Prince Charles with a job which consists of little more than wandering around, being charming, and shaking people by the hand. There are many who would find this kind of life deadening, but fate has been more than kind to Prince Charles and has provided him with an animal sign which is to the manor born. On the whole, Rats love nothing more than a gentle stroll through life, making the least number of plans for the future and enjoying their highly developed senses to the full. Judging from his performance so far, Prince Charles would seem to be no exception. The Rat's personality is tailor-made for royalty and it is perhaps more than mere coincidence that, apart from Dragons, they far outnumber all other signs. Prince Henry, the Queen Mother, Prince Andrew and Princess Alexandra are among those who were all born in a Rat year. There are in fact, no less than six Rats in the present Royal Family.

If the undercurrent of aggression that exists by degrees in all Rats sometimes leads easy-going extraverts to turn inwards, urging them to plan life as if it were a military exercise, clearly this is not true of the Prince of Wales. Charles is an extravert at heart, with a positive outlook. But as we shall see, Britain's future monarch, although an open-minded and passionate Rat, does have problems. And most of these are bound up with both the positive and negative sides of his animal sign.

Early years

The year of Charles's birth, 1948, provided a constant stream of examples of the Rat's warm-hearted but restless influence. And their opportunist nature was never far from view. Typically, it was the year bread rationing came to an end. It was also the year the historic Berlin Airlift was put into operation, sending much needed supplies to American and British zones in Berlin. The Rat year of 1948 also saw electricity nationalized, the state of Israel and the Republic of Korea proclaimed. In November, Harry S. Truman was elected president of the United States with the smallest number of votes ever recorded. And considering it was the Rat's influence that held sway, the hit song of the year could not have been more appropriate—'All I Want For Christmas is My Two Front Teeth'!

The Chinese say that of the Rat's three stages of life, the first, childhood and early adolescence, is the easiest. Put another way, it might be said that a Rat's school days are truly the happiest.

Certainly, the Prince of Wales enjoyed a blissfully easy early stage, although there was one anxious moment early on for the young and hungry royal Rat—he was issued with a ration book! Like most royal children, Charles was protected by nannies while his parents travelled abroad. Not unnaturally, this closeted existence provided him with a somewhat limited view of the outside world. Aged 8, he asked, with not a little of the Rat's natural inquisitiveness, 'Mummy what *are* schoolboys?' Charles was soon to find out when he became the first heir to the throne to go to school. Charles went first to the then recently opened Hill House School in Knightsbridge. He spent only two terms there before going from one of the newest schools to one of the oldest, Cheam Preparatory School, in Berkshire. His father, Prince Philip had once studied here, and so had Winston Churchill. Charles once summed up his early experiences as a schoolboy: 'I suppose I could have gone to the local comprehensive or the local grammar,' he said, 'but I am not sure it would have done me much good. You learn, they say, the way a monkey learns: watching its parents! On the whole, you pick it up as you go along.' It is a statement which demonstrates much of the Rat's perception and objectivity.

Although it is the case that monkeys—including those born in the Monkey year—tend to learn by imitating, it is not always strictly true of Rat children. Rats require parents with animal signs whose influence is both strong and warm-hearted if they are to discover ways of keeping their sometimes fatal opportunism in check. Charles has been only half fortunate in respect of his parents' signs. Both his Rooster father and his Tiger mother have very strong notions about the way children should be educated, but the Chinese Horoscope would point out that they do not always see eye to eye on how this should best be achieved. Rooster fathers are usually old-fashioned fundamentalists who lack compassion. On the other hand, the Tiger mother will teach by example and has a mind open to new ideas. Charles's education was obviously a compromise, ending up a mixture of both Tiger's and Rooster's strongest wishes. However, the next choice of school was clearly that of the Rooster. In May 1962 (the year of the Rat's great enemy the Tiger) Charles was packed off to his father's old seat of learning—Gordonstoun. The emphasis there was on tough outdoor living, stressing the importance of 'character' and 'initiative'. Days began with a run around the garden followed by a cold shower. Rats are extremely quick to learn and young Rats enjoy all subjects which stimulate their active minds and bodies. While at Gordonstoun, the Prince learned to drive, play polo, sail and water-ski. He also shot his first stag—a questionable outlet for his Rat's aggressive instincts and one which Charles has used throughout his life to let off steam.

His academic achievements at Gordonstoun were average but the Prince managed O level passes in English language and English literature, subjects that Rat children would seem to prefer. Throughout history, Rat people have distinguished themselves in the arts, especially literature. Shakespeare and Tolstoy were both born in a Rat year, as were Charlotte Brontë, James Baldwin, Raymond Chandler, Robert Bolt, Lawrence Durrell, and so the list goes on. By no stretch of the imagination could Charles be considered a full-time writer, but writing is a craft he clearly feels at home with. He has published one widely praised children's story, *The Old Man of Lochnagar*, he is the first royal to review a book for *Punch* and it is understood that Prince Charles writes his own speeches. The Prince also passed in History, French and Latin but fell down on maths, maybe a problem subject for all Rats unless there is a financial deal involved.

While at Gordonstoun, there was an occasion which fully illustrated the Rat's emerging nature—love of life and unquenchable desire to experience it to the full. On a school sailing trip around the Hebrides, the young Prince lost his police escort, went into a pub and drank a glass of cherry brandy. The Rat has a monstrously sweet tooth (for example, the animals only eat the refined, sweeter-tasting white rice) and as his animal decrees, Charles would see nothing wrong in downing a large cherry brandy—even at the tender age of 14. The incident made international headlines and the Prince of Wales's recollection of that famous event contains another key feature of the Rat personality—the Rat's ready wit. 'Having never been into a bar before,' he recalls, 'the first think I thought of doing was having a drink. Well, I thought it was the end of the earth. I was all ready to pack my bags and leave for Siberia.'

Prince Charles's next school wasn't exactly Siberia. It was, in fact, a lot further and in some ways just as unpleasant, especially for the home-loving Rat who places such a high premium on comfort. The next educational stop was Timbertop, the annex of Geelong Church of England School, situated in the wooded mountains north-east of Melbourne.

Another strong indication of the Rat's influence is to be found when things go wrong. Here a Rat will be the first to grumble and a really bad reversal sees them fretting endlessly over trivialities. There was more than a little of the grumbling Rat when Charles spoke of the two terms he spent in Australia. 'It was ninety degrees in the shade,' he said, 'with flies everywhere, and you sort of ran around amongst the kangaroos and things. Dust and everything.' But Timbertop wasn't all bad and Prince Charles once described his time there as 'The most wonderful experience I've ever had, I think'.

The Prince of Wales was much more positive about his years at Trinity. Following another year at Gordonstoun, where he learned the 'cello and played the lead role in *Macbeth*, Charles went to Cambridge. He was 19, and at an age when young people begin to stand on their own two feet. At university, Charles's Rat personality was freer to express itself than at any time hitherto. Of all the 12 signs of the Chinese Horoscope, no other animal has a broader intellectual horizon. Rats have a quick mind and, although they often prefer to let others toil on their behalf, once they set their sights on a goal, they go about achieving it with a tenacious enthusiasm.

As well as possessing the gift for literature, Rats also excel in the fields of music, history, and humour. History in particular— digging up long-forgotten material and sifting through conflicting reports—is greatly simplified by the Rat's skill of facing most matters objectively. At Trinity College, Charles would seem to have let his influencing animal dictate the choice of subjects. The first year he studied archaeology and anthropology and later switched to a two-year honours course in history. Charles said, 'I've always been interested in history, even when I was quite small. I don't know whether it's me or being born into what I was, but I *feel* history.'

Being the first in line is very Rat-like and it has been a marked feature of the Prince of Wales. Remember that in the legend which explains the origin of the Chinese Horoscopes, when the Buddha invited all the animals to join him for the New Year celebration, the Rat arrived first by leaping over the Buffalo's back. Again and again while examining his life, I found the phrase 'the first heir to the throne to do such a thing', constantly recurring. A perfect example of this happened in June 1970, when Prince Charles became the first heir apparent to obtain a degree—a second class B.A. The feeling is that he would have done better if he had worked harder, but given the sensuous nature of the Rat, Charles had other plans. 'Maximum pleasure with minimum effort' is the code of most Rats and it was away from the study that Charles's Rat character showed itself most clearly. 'Half the fun at Cambridge is to climb in all hours of the day and night,' he once admitted. Charles later added, with more than a hint of the Rat's sexual openness, 'The guest hours have been lengthened and you can have a girl or anybody else in your room until two o'clock in the morning'. Judging by his success with ladies in later years, 'anybody else' was a phrase tagged on to keep the press from making a meal of his statement. But the press are never far away from the future King and one of the many girls reported to have stayed till the stroke of two was Sybilla Dorman.

Daughter of the former Governor-General of Malta, Sybilla was born in a Buffalo year, 1949 (a generation older than his future wife). Both she and Charles were reading history and shared a fondness of amateur dramatics. They also shared a holiday in Malta. However, Sybilla wasn't Charles's first love at Cambridge. This was to be Lucia Santa Cruz, three years older than Charles and therefore born in a Rooster year. He was clearly smitten by Lucia, but Roosters are not creatures who indulge in casual romance. The affair was important to Charles, his first Big Romance, but it wasn't to last. Rats and Roosters do not mix comfortably and rate zero marks for a lasting understanding at practically every level.

An an undergraduate, Charles found an outlet for the humorous as well as the sensual side of his nature. The Rat's sharp wit cannot be stressed often enough and with their love of society and excitement it is not unusual to find the theatrical world teeming with Rat people. At Cambridge, Charles developed a talent for comedy and performed in a satirical review. In one sketch he ended up having a custard pie thrown in his face (not real custard, unfortunately for the Rat) and in the Cambridge Footlights Review he played a singing dustman. His love of the Goons, which he discovered long after their radio show had ceased, was and still remains the heart of his humour.

Middle years

For all Rats, the middle period of life is the one that presents most problems. They have a restless temperament, which normally means that the pillars of a stable life—a secure home and careful financial investment—tend to suffer. Obviously, Prince Charles has no money worries but as we will discover, his domestic set-up leaves a lot to be desired.

Charles's first public step into manhood was his investiture as the Prince of Wales, at Caernarfon Castle on 1 July 1969—the Year of the Rooster as it happened. The Chinese say that the Rooster is the animal sign most associated with military parades and dressing up in uniforms; their fine plumage has much to do with this belief. Charles clearly went along with the Rooster's notion of making the historic event worthwhile. He said at the time 'If you're going to have a ceremony like this, you should spend enough money to make it dignified, colourful, and worthy of Britain'. As one might expect, the Prince met the occasion in full command of his Rat's charm. His comment after was 'I met so many people and waved so much I woke up in the middle of the night waving my hand'. Although he didn't dress up in pantaloons like the Duke of Windsor at his investiture, Prince Charles made a great impression. In spite of the Welsh nationalists and their bomb campaign, the investiture was a great success, seen by over 500 million people on television. But if Charles was reluctant to dress up for his investiture, his next jobs provided no escape.

Two activities dominated Prince Charles's public life during the seventies: his period in the services and his role as ambassador. Both jobs are connected and combine perfectly to suit the Rat's many-sided temperament. His life in the services particularly appealed to that side of the Rat which is eager for new experiences. He served in the Navy and the RAF, but, of the two, it is clear that the RAF held the greater attraction. Rats love to experience all their senses, and the more they can enjoy at once, the happier they are. Flying an aircraft is tailor-made for the sense-hungry Rat and Prince Charles took to the air as ducks take to water. The water, by the way was not for Charles, although he was made a Companion of the Grand Order of Water Rats. As he explained after 10 weeks of his first naval command: 'They took ten years off my life . . . I feel about eighty'. The air was another matter. He said 'If you're living dangerously, it tends to make you appreciate life that much more and want to live it to the fullest. If you do make a mistake, your life often depends on taking the correct action immediately. It's very challenging. There's that superb mixture and fear and enjoyment which overcomes me.' Such comments are straight from the text book of the Rat's personality.

During his life the Prince has found an absorbing interest in the arts, and like his predecessor, Charles I, who was also a Rat, he has been a keen collector. The future Charles III says that he has collected over 100 loo seats and all offers of more are welcome. Before he was married, Charles had collected a large number of trolls, which he sported on his mantelpiece. Diana, it seemed, did not like trolls and friends say they have long since disappeared.

But Charles does have a more serious concern for the arts—he plays the 'cello, paints attractive watercolours, acted as a student (he once came on stage with an umbrella and said 'I lead a sheltered life'), writes, and supports traditional architecture. On the other hand, taking things up is definitely a Rat feature, and one which is again typified by the Prince of Wales. He once admitted 'I am one of those people who leaps from one thing to another'. It is an admission that would serve as a maxim for a Rat, no matter what their position on the social scale.

In sport, too, Charles has tended to leap from one activity to the other. A very short list shows that he has parachuted, dived to the ocean's bed, skied, windsurfed, ridden a skateboard, and played polo, a game he loves. It is also the one game he has worked at to improve. Like shooting, thumping a wooden ball about with a mallet while riding a horse brings into play many senses at once, and it is not surprising to find the Rat's undercurrent of aggression released as a result. Certainly this is true of Prince Charles.

There is no Rat on earth who can resist the promise that travel brings: the thrill of new places, new smells, new faces, new food, new everything! Not uncharacteristically, Charles has seen a fair bit of the world, and not just that part of it over which he will one day rule. At no other time does his Rat-inspired wit make itself more obvious than when on tour. Relaxed away from his chores at home, sun, sea and an ever-increasing number of young ladies who fling themselves at him for a swift embrace, provide Charles with just the right backdrop for some of his wittiest comments. Here are a few pearls reminding us of how spontaneous the Rat personality can be. On Australia: 'A funny thing happened—I made a mistake and got off the plane'. In Bermuda he said: 'Bearing in mind I am the first Charles to have anything to do with a parliament for 350 years, I might have turned nasty and dissolved you'. Asked if he was touched by visiting the Taj Mahal, he replied: "Well, I did bang my head against the ceiling at one point'. On the same trip he made a telling comment, one which does speak oceans about his Rat sign. He said: 'A marvellous idea, to build something so wonderful . . . to someone one loved so much'.

Love, in all its forms, features strongly in the life of Rat people and they find falling in love remarkably easy. Once given, Rats find their love for someone impossible to give up. Rats do not like giving anything up once they have taken it on board. Diets and self-denial are definitely not for Rats. As we have seen, art, history, and sport, may all feature strongly in a Rat's life, and have certainly done so in the case of Prince Charles. But the Rat's warm and never less than passionate heart provides the clearest clue as to their governing sign. Considering the restrictions imposed on him as a result of being the future King, Charles has had remarkable success in finding partners to share his obviously pronounced sexual feelings. Blue-blooded he may be in *Debrett*, but it is his Rat's sign that ensures that red blood courses through His Royal Highness's veins. Before he met Lady Diana Spencer, Charles's name was linked with a long list of potential brides who, for reasons which ranged from being a Catholic to not being a virgin, were considered unsuitable. The roll-call of ships that passed in the royal night is pretty impressive, even by a Rat's standards. It includes: Lady Leonora Grosvenor, Lady Jane Grosvenor, Lady Victoria Percy, Lady Caroline Percy, Bettina Lindsay, Lady Cecil Kerr, Lady Henrietta Fitzroy, Lady Charlotte Manners, and Lady Camilla Fane. Insiders say that Charles fell deeply for all those who were to share the biggest headlines, and it must be said than when viewing them in terms of their animal sign, several would appear to have had a much greater long-term compatibility than the lady with whom he finally walked down the aisle.

Charles once said 'In many cases, one falls madly in "love" with somebody with whom you are infatuated rather than in love'. Of all the women who Charles fell 'madly' for, it is commonly thought that Lady Jane Wellesley was one who would have been ideally suited. The Chinese Horoscopes would disagree. Lady Jane was born on 6 July, 1951, which makes her sign the Cat. It is universally known that Cats eat Rats, and their compatibility rating is one out of five stars for romance and zero in marriage. Davina Sheffield was another Cat lady for whom Charles could not disguise his feelings, and this affair too turned sour. The same compatibility rating is true of Princess Marie Astrid, who was born in 1954—a Horse year. Rats and Horses are non-starters. There are not many marks either for a Rat and Rooster, which put Lady Amanda Knatchbull (born 1957) out of the picture. But it is not all gloom for the Rat who wishes to be wed—far from it. The ideal marriage partner for a Rat is a Dragon, but there is no evidence that Charles met one. A perfectly acceptable alternative to the Dragon is a Goat. Both Sabrina Guiness and Lady Sarah Spencer were born in a Goat year—1955. Although Rats and Goats get no points in love, their prospects of harmony and a long life together improve dramatically once the marriage knot is tied; then they score a maximum. The converse is true of the Rat and Princess Diana's sign—the Buffalo. Rats are inescapably attracted to the Buffalo sign. The reason for this fascination is the classic attraction of opposites, for it is a fact that Rat and Buffalo have little or nothing in common. But whereas romance between the two signs is usually a glittering success, practically all Rat and Buffalo marriages tend to end in disaster.

The future

The greatest influence outside his parental home was great uncle Louis (born 25 June 1900), whose Rat qualities of warmth, social ease and generosity have helped Charles to come to terms with his public identity. It was almost certainly because of their close and long-lasting relationship that Charles is able to say: 'Were it not for my ability to see the funny side of my life, I'd have been committed to an institution long ago'. For spiritual guidance, Charles has kept the company of Laurens Van der Post, a student of the great Swiss psychologist Carl Jung. Van der Post was born on 13 December 1906, which makes him a Horse. Rats and Horses have little understanding and one cannot doubt that most of Charles's more eccentric ideas—his quasi-vegetarianism, talking to plants, and interest in the occult are due to Van der Post's less-than-auspicious influence. A more healthy relationship was that forged with Sir John Higgs, a member of Charles's staff and an expert on farming and estate management. Sir John was born in the Year of the Pig, and Rats and Pigs have a very close understanding. In fact, Prince Charles knighted Sir John on his deathbed. No such happy relationship existed with Edward Adeane who left Charles's service after a blazing row. Adeane, Charles's extremely efficient private secretary and treasurer from 1979, was born on 4 October 1939, the Year of the Cat. It cannot be stressed often enough that Cats and Rats make poor companions.

Although quick to flatter, the Rat is not easily flattered in return. This helps to keep a clear head on the Rat's shoulders and the Chinese say that a Rat's advice is worth taking. Given that he is married to a Buffalo, a creature who will dominate any partner with the possible exclusion of the Dragon, Charles will have to fight to get his advice heard. It may transpire that the Prince will be left to act out the long-established Buddhist concept which he mentioned when interviewed with his wife on TV. 'I just feel sometimes I can throw a rock into a pond and watch the ripples create a certain amount of discussion'.

While waiting to be crowned, Prince Charles should find his position as someone without a definite role more and more acceptable. The Chinese Horoscopes say that Rats can look forward to a contented old age, but must face the possibility of a sudden end (Charles I and Lord Louis Mountbatten were both Rats for whom this proved to be the case). If the headline of *The Times* of Friday 12 March 1988 was to be believed, Prince Charles was, 'feet from death' when an avalanche killed his friend, Major Hugh Lindsay. The exact distance is in dispute, but there can be little doubt that the Prince was indeed very close to being engulfed in the torrent of snow and ice that suddenly and without warning swept down the infamous Wang slope in the Swiss skiing resort of Klosters. As the Chinese repeatedly point out, the year of the Dragon invariably begins and ends with a disaster of major proportions. To have lost the future King of England in an avalanche would have proved the prophesy true, unthinkable though it may be. But the fact is that Charles survived by the narrowest of margins and it is right that the Chinese Horoscopes be questioned. Needless to say, they are not silent on such an event. Charles is a Rat, and as such enjoys huge success in a Dragon year, perhaps more than any other. Under the laws that govern the Chinese Horoscope a main feature to be considered here is the all-powerful Dragon's luck, the quality most pronounced in a Dragon year. The Chinese would say it was this factor alone which was responsible for Charles being 'feet from death' when the avalanche struck. And the whole incident reveals much about Charles and his influencing sign. After the accident, Charles gave a written statement which highlighted two main elements of the Rat's influence, their delight in danger and the total objectivity with which they can judge even the most tragic events. 'There is a special dimension to skiing off piste,' he said, 'which is hard to describe to those who have not experienced it or do not wish to.' He went on, 'Avalanches are a natural phenomenon of the mountains and when it comes to avoiding them no one is infallible,'

But with a disaster consisting, one hopes, of no more than a fanciful omen, Charles's mentors will continue to put him in the right frame of mind for doing little more than pottering around the farm at Highgrove and telling the BMA to take homoeopathic medicine seriously. Yet there is a sense in which Charles needs to do more, to impress us all that he has something else to offer than mere charm. In the early weeks of 1988 he again made headlines with a controversial statement—one of an increasing number of such statements. The Prince told a private dinner party he wished he were more like Bob Geldof, a desire held, on the face of it, by a great many who wish to see an end to starvation. The press had a field day, but as usual missed the point. Charles was simply saying, in so many words, that his Chinese sign demands a greater freedom to act in accordance with deep seated passions. Rats may be restless, poor timekeepers and opportunist, but no one is more open-minded or generous. Seen in this light, it could be said that a contented Rat means plenty for all. Waiting to be King *can* offer ways to fulfil a Rat's needs but, as we have seen, it may equally provide almost as many obstacles.

In his early thirties, Prince Charles said, 'I might not be King for 40 years, so I don't know what my role will be'. It is sometimes painfully obvious that as long as he searches, the Rat Prince will not be happy. The moment he realises, as he does from time to time, that the clue to his job is to be found through his influencing animal's gifts, the future will look less bleak and life less frustrating. The charming Rat, in every sense, becomes our real-life Prince Charming.

The Princess of Wales
Birthdate: 1 July 1961
Born in the Year of the Buffalo

Writing in the sixteenth century, the naturalist and vicar the Reverend Topsell described the Buffalo as, 'a simple beast, though his aspect seems to be grave'. Simple the Buffalo is not, although I would concede, and so would the Chinese Horoscopes, that those born under this powerful animal's sign are frequently solemn. No other animal has done more to change the face of the planet on which we live. In the arts, in politics, in war, the Buffalo stands shoulder high above all others. They are born under the twin signs of tenacity and endurance, and when given the world stage to perform on, the Buffalo stands in the centre and gives way to no one. They are beasts who are born to lead and frequently do so. The Buffalo is boss and power sharing is out of the question. Bearing this in mind, Princess Diana's astonishing rise to world fame and popularity is that much more comprehensible. As a fashion leader she is in a class of her own and what she wears today, the world wears tomorrow. If her face appears on the front of a magazine, from *Woman* to *Nursing Times*, it will sell thousands of extra copies. In less than a decade, Diana has risen from the obscurity of teaching in a Pimlico kindergarten to being arguably the most influential woman of her generation.

Early years

The year of Diana's birth, 1961, was in many ways a classic in terms of the Buffalo influence. The Chinese hold that this is not a period for deadbeats and layabouts. Political revolution is common, with world leaderships constantly under threat. 1961 saw the sudden deaths of Dag Hammarskjöld, the highly respected secretary general of the United Nations, and King Mohammed V of Morocco. In Russia, Stalin's body was removed from the Lenin Mausoleum in Red Square and the day after Diana was born, 2 July, Ernest Hemingway was found dead from a self-inflicted gun shot. Moreover, a Buffalo year is a time for justice, as the trial and subsequent conviction of Nazi war criminal, Adolf Eichmann dramatically illustrated.

The Chinese Horoscopes point out that Buffalo people will suffer a difficult early period and that childhood will find them prone to long periods of isolation. Secretive as a child, frequently stubborn, and poor at revealing her inner feelings, Diana was typical of her influencing animal. Although they usually fight shy of displays of physical love, Buffalo children require a great deal of understanding from their parents in order to overcome an extremely complex temperament. Diana was unlucky from this point of view. In 1967, the Year of the ever-capricious Goat, her mother and father (the eighth Earl Spencer) separated, divorcing two years later in the Year of the no-nonsense Rooster. Diana coped with the sadness, first by keeping her self very much to herself but later finding an outlet for her unhappiness by mothering her younger brother Charles, born in the Dragon year of 1964. Buffaloes make strict but fair parents and a Buffalo mother will often express her commitment to family life at an early age. Clearly, Diana's behaviour at that crucial period of growing up bears this out. Along with her surrogate motherhood, Diana's character never deviated from the single-mindedness of her influencing animal. 'Diana was sweet,' says her stepmother, Raine Spencer, who was not accepted easily by the Earl's children, 'but she always did her own thing.'

But if Princess Diana was unlucky that her father's first wife was not compatible, the sign of his second choice is quite another matter. The Earl is a Pig, born on 24 January 1924 and the Countess Spencer a Snake, her birthday being 9 September 1929. The Chinese Horoscopes give four out of five stars for a Pig and Snake marriage and there can be no doubting the devotion showed by Raine Spencer to her husband, especially after his brain haemorrhage. Diana's stepmother bought a degree of stability to the Spencer home and so provided the teenage Lady Di with a firmer platform from which to launch herself into womanhood. This she has done with breathtaking ease, largely due to a characteristic of the Buffalo which is highly pronounced in Diana and not always given a chance to express itself in all females of the sign. The quality here is her ability to dress up to kill—to 'knock 'em dead', as they used to say. No one does this to greater effect than the Princess of Wales.

The Chinese Horoscopes reveal that Buffalo women are practical and unfussy in their dress. Although normally unconcerned with fashion, Buffalo ladies really go to town when the need arises—which in Princess Diana's case is most days and nights. Asked to put on a show, the Buffalo lady is capable of dressing better than almost any other female, and she has plenty of fashionable rivals—the Horse, the Cat, and the Goat among them. Not unexpectedly, the world's most influential models over the last two decades, Twiggy and Jean Shrimpton, are a Buffalo and a Horse, respectively. At all times, Buffaloes are, in a sense, driven by the need to run the world their way. From small daily domestic decisions to major events, Buffaloes demand that their often unique voice be both heard and heeded. To this somewhat daunting end, making a visual impression that lasts is clearly essential. For a Buffalo lady this will often take the form of looking absolutely immaculate. Fired by a powerful inner conviction, the Buffalo influence demands an exterior to match. As a result, she will always present herself with classic elegance, itself an expression of her deep-rooted conservatism. Princess Diana's choice of Elizabeth and David Emanuel to design her wedding dress illustrates this point perfectly. The Emanuels are classic designers who draw much of their inspiration from the Victorian period, one which today evokes sophistication and assurance— twin characteristics of the female Buffalo at one with herself. In a nutshell, Princess Diana dresses fashionably but never follows the trend. To do so is definitely *not* a Buffalo trait. But to say that she *creates* trends is, of course, quite another matter.

Middle years

Such is the Buffalo's influence, 'predicting' the future of an individual as positive and deliberate as Princess Diana is comparatively easy. Unlike some animal signs, who chop and change, the Buffalo character is set at birth and few, if any, deviate. Once familiar with his or her own field, the Buffalo will plough it relentlessly. However, all periods of Buffaloes lives are largely determined by how successfully they off-set their inner convictions against an eternally complex heart. And the Buffalo finds times when such internal wars are lost, in spite of great struggles.

The most common problem period for a Buffalo is mid life. During this phase, the Chinese warn, Buffaloes are more likely to suffer from a broken marriage than any other animal sign. The reason for this all-too-common state of affairs is located in the root of their deep and complex heart. Driven by inner forces that they can never fully come to terms with, Buffalo people all too frequently end up blaming those closest to them for their own 'weaknesses'. These, of course, are only weaknesses as judged by their own impossibly high, and sometimes eccentric, standards. This makes living with a Buffalo an often painful experience. Buffaloes rule in the home, and what they say goes. In the years she has been married to Prince Charles, Diana has made it clear that her wishes are those that are to be obeyed. The Palace's public relations machine is eager to play down this side of their most popular property, Chuck and Di, but the stories get out. Diana has been quite ruthless in weeding out what she considers undesirable influences. 'How can anyone call her coy?' says Charles's ex-valet, Stephen Barry. 'How can anyone believe all that sugary stuff about her. She hires and fires with the best of them and is very demanding. She is a tremendous fighter.' (We should remind ourselves here, that Mrs Thatcher, Hitler, and Napoleon were all born in the Year of the Buffalo.)

The future

The Chinese say that old age finds Buffaloes often on their own, solitary, rather sad creatures who sit regretting the muddles that their complex nature has created. Most of their friends will have grown tired of the Buffalo's demanding ways and their determination to be right at all times. By the time they reach their final phase, all but the most devoted and loyal will have been alienated. Relatives, while admiring the sad old animal's former glories—of which there will be a great many—will not be eager to share the Buffalo's bitterness and, in extreme cases, self-pity. Unfortunately for Diana, her closest relatives, at least those who are most likely to survive with her, are not at all compatible. In fact, they are poles apart.

The Chinese are uniquely specific in their compatibility charts of animal signs and they explain that the Buffalo has few really close allies, neither as friends or relatives. In Diana's case, the family she has married into are considered mainly unsuitable. Buffaloes and Tigers, for example, get the lowest rating of *any animal combination*. This means that Diana, her mother-in-law, the Queen (a Tiger, born 21 April 1926), and her sister-in-law, Anne (a Tiger, born 15 August 1950), will not be seeing a lot of each other, now or in the future. The Buffalo, it is said, grinds the Tiger down and my own experience of the Chinese Horoscopes has seen this proved time and again. Diana will, on the other hand, be a good aunt to Anne's daughter, Zara (born 15 May 1981). Zara is a Rooster, which is just about the only sign to hit it off with the often solitary Buffalo. They are both conservative creatures and are usually found sharing a love of the country and all its traditions. The Duke of Edinburgh (born 10 June 1921) is also a Rooster, and it is not surprising to learn that Royal Watchers say he is one member of the Windsor home with whom Diana feels an affinity. She also get on well with the Duchess of York, in spite of silly attempts by some sections of the press to prove otherwise. Fergie is a Pig (born 15 October 1959), and Pigs and Buffaloes get four out of five stars for friendship. Pigs are cheerful and uncomplicated, and because they tend to lack initiative Pigs work well in partnerships, instilling confidence in others and displaying great loyalty. Before her romance with Prince Andrew, Fergie was regularly summoned to the Palace in an effort to cheer up Diana during one of her, then more common, periodic spells of inner uncertainty. The Chinese Horoscopes predict a lasting relationship between Diana and Sarah, and I see no reason to contradict them.

In old age, Buffaloes have a tendency to go to seed. But such an end can be avoided and Buffalo ladies in particular have an escape route. This takes the shape of a single-minded devotion to family life and the home. Gardening, making clothes, baking cakes are all activities which provide the Buffalo's frequently tormented soul with a soothing outlet. But domesticity of this kind is not the lot of a beautiful princess, especially if she happens to be married to the eldest son of, among other titles, the richest woman in the world. For a Buffalo in Diana's unique position, salvation will almost certainly be found in dealing with her own children and the disadvantaged she meets outside Highgrove. Diana has, in fact, already made important steps in this direction. On television she indicated that she'd been impressed by the work of the hospices for the terminally ill. 'After I had been around the first ward,' she said, 'I was struck by the calmness of the patients confronting their illness. They were so brave about it and made me feel so humble.' This is a good omen for Diana's future. The word 'humble' does not come easily to a Buffalo's lips and it indicates a willingness to be part of, rather than running, the show. Later in the same interview, Diana made another telling comment: 'I don't know how I could cope if I had a child who was handicapped or mentally handicapped in some way,' she admitted openly, 'So I'm going out there to meet these children, and I'm learning all the time and trying desperately to understand how they cope.' Again this is typical of a Buffalo treading the right path—the one that leads to self-awareness.

As she grows older, Diana will have to deal more and more with the complexities that flow from her influencing animal. The evidence so far is that in spite of the fun-loving, pop-fan image created by those on the outside, Princess Diana is very much in control of her own considerable destiny. 'Nothing would upset me more,' she once said, her Buffalo sign well to the fore, 'than just being a name on top of a piece of paper.' There will be no such upsets for the Princess of Wales. In less than a decade she has risen to the very top of the social scale and might easily be described as the most popular woman in the world.

The Prince and Princess of Wales as marriage partners

The Rat and the Buffalo, Charles's and Diana's signs, are chalk and cheese. But as with all attractions of opposites, the heady days of new love frequently promise more than they can ever possibly deliver. Buffaloes and Rats are frequently fiercely attracted to each other in the early stages of an affair. The Rat is quickly seduced by the Buffalo's strong personality, and the Buffalo is invariably excited by the Rat's sensual charm. But marriage is a different matter. Whereas in romance, Rats and Buffaloes are given a very high rating, they score not one point when married. The Buffalo quickly assumes control and the free-wheeling Rat is left either to comply or get out.

There can be little doubt that Charles and Diana were deeply in love when they first met, and I believe it is true to say that the world at large was in some way uplifted by their blossoming affair. But it wasn't all romance. Buffaloes are world leaders who once they have set their heart and mind on a goal do not give up easily. With the promise of a chance to share the throne, Diana was determined to make sure she was not going to end up as just another name in Charles's long list of conquests. On the surface, Diana is all shyness and blushes but her Buffalo influence is never far away. She met Charles when she was only sixteen and decided then he was the man she wanted to marry. In keeping with her animal sign, Diana played the waiting game with commendable skill, witness the expert manner with which she handled the press and publicity during her courtship and engagement.

From Charles's point of view, his choice of bride was more or less determined by the need to marry a virgin. In a permissive society like ours, this proved to be a bigger task than it had first appeared. Diana clearly had no black marks against her in this respect and since they were evidently in love, marriage was the obvious next step. But the good news ends there. The Prince and Princess of Wales, a Rat and a Buffalo joined in holy matrimony are not compatible. In spite of the fact that there are sections of the press who, for reasons of pure sensationalism, wish to make the marriage appear in a worse state, it cannot be stated too strongly that in partnership—for that's what most marriages need to become in order to survive—the Buffalo cannot avoid trying to dominate the Rat. The result is that the Rat, in this case Prince Charles, becomes more and more isolated from his instinctive and sensual approach to life. Under the determined and stubborn Buffalo, the Rat either turns inward to escape, or simply bolts down the first hole.

The often overworked Palace press office is quick to scotch rumours that all is not well at the Wales's Highgrove home. Their explanation for all reported 'rifts' is that two people of different age groups usually enjoy separate activities and friends. But this somewhat lame excuse does not fit in with the facts. Lots of couples marry with a 13-year gap between their ages and live happily sharing the same holidays, friends, and pastimes. But this is not the case when one is a Rat and the other a Buffalo. The blunt truth is that the Chinese signs handed to Charles and Diana in the years of their births have no common ground intellectually, spiritually, or emotionally and their lack of shared tastes is merely highlighted by their respective animal influences. Charles's solitary trips to Scotland, his interest in the spiritual world, his genuine love of painting and classical music are not just symptoms of a growing apart from Diana, they are the cause. In turn, her deeply felt but simple attitudes are a part of another, quite separate plan.

Charles was born to rule, it is his birthright. That he was born in the year of the Rat should make his role as monarch both rich and rewarding. Diana, on the other hand, has built her position from almost nothing. This she has done with the aid of a cloaked tenacity. It is the iron fist in a velvet glove, the most powerful and effective of all the Buffalo's many weapons. But there is a negative side to world leadership. As Buffaloes grow older and more confident, they become rigid in their thinking. With the march of time, Princess Diana will appear markedly conservative in her behaviour. She will become stubborn in the face of criticism and take advice from fewer and fewer friends. Charles's future life will be quite the reverse. The Rat's open mind will want greater freedom and his senses will demand a deeper appreciation than that offered by his steadily more intolerant Buffalo wife. In short, what Prince Charles needed was a partner capable of enjoying the Rat's ready wit and keen intelligence, someone to bend with the changing winds life brings. Instead, the future King of England has married one of the world's most beautiful, determined, and ambitious Buffalo women.

The Prince and Princess of Wales as parents

Generally speaking, both Rats and Buffaloes make excellent parents but as in practically everything else, their methods are totally opposed. The Rat parent, especially a male Rat tends to let his warmth and sense of humour govern his style. Rats normally place great emphasis on a broad education and unless the Rat in question is the introverted plan maker, they do not exercise discipline for its own sake. Clearly, Prince Charles has not yet decided about his children's long-term education: 'I think it's too soon really,' he says, 'There's no hurry at all until we see what sort of characters they are going to produce as they get older, and then we can find a school they can adjust to.'

On the negative side, Charles might well fret over trivialities and the permanent undercurrent of aggression that bedevils all Rats could easily spill out in the face of a child's slowness to learn. Buffaloes, on the other hand, view parenthood as they do all things and demand discipline from an early age. Even so, Buffalo parents usually remain calm in a crisis. They tend to rule their children with an iron rod and a Buffalo mother is tireless in her efforts to ensure that her offspring have the best possible ducation (reading, writing, and arithmetic). In short, the Rat rushes headlong at parenthood, while the Buffalo steps back and deliberates long and hard. It was Prince Charles who got William used to having baths by climbing in with him.

Prince William of Wales
Birthdate: 21 June 1982
Born in the Year of the Dog

Prince Henry of Wales
Birthdate: 15 September 1984
Born in the Year of the Rat

So far as Charles's and Diana's children are concerned, Harry and Wills have animal signs which are auspicious to a marked degree. Prince William is a Dog, and Prince Harry a Rat, like his father. Dogs and Rats are easily understood by a Rat father and both signs score four out of five stars for compatibility with a Rat parent. Diana's sign makes her less compatible with her offspring. Although she scores the same high points as Charles for understanding Harry the Rat, Wills the Dog and his Buffalo mum have nothing in common. In fact, the Chinese Horoscopes show that Dog and Buffalo get no points for compatibility. The Dog's great confederate in life is the Tiger, with whom they get on extremely well. Dogs and Tigers have an understanding which is based on a form of idealism, and they tend to strive for a better world. The Queen and Princess Anne are both Tigers, which suggests the perfect favourite aunt and grandmother syndrome for the young Prince William. But Diana is a devoted parent and her influencing animal will dictate that she'll do everything possible to ensure that her children grow up with an appreciation of life's traditional virtues.

Barring unthinkable disasters, William will one day succeed to the English throne. Should this happy event take place, William will be the first Dog in our long history to do so. Once they set their minds on a task, Dogs never give up. With their outstanding sense of loyalty and devotion to a worthwhile cause, Dogs make first-rate leaders. They cheer for the underdog and I fully expect

William to grow into an idealist King. But the one danger which faces Dog people, as well as the four-legged variety, is too much pampering. A child who is born to be King can often be spoiled, which in Dog sign terms means a tendency towards stubbornness and over anxiety.

In terms of a marriage partner, the Chinese Horoscopes would point to William marrying a Tiger, like his grandmother Elizabeth and Aunt Anne. He may also find his Aunt Sarah, a Pig, sympathetic, another auspicious sign for the male Dog. A Rat like his father, Prince Harry might well seek a Pig for a bride, having almost certainly rejected the sign of his Buffalo mother. Harry is not likely to follow in his father's footsteps and marry as a result of an infatuation. But it must always be remembered that Rats and Buffaloes present a powerful attraction of opposites.

In common with his Uncle Andrew, with little thought of ever becoming King, Harry will very likely join the services. It provides the sensation-seeking Rat with a ready-made social life and not a great deal of work. Service life offers free travel and a happy mixture of easy-going routine and comfort—especially if the Rat in question is a member of the Royal Family. Whereas Andrew and Charles share much as a result of their influencing animal sign—two Rats tend to be good chums—Harry and Wills have nothing to keep them together. Even so, it should be underlined that the Dog's loyalty to the Rat will seldom, if ever, be questioned and it is my considered view that during his lifetime, there will be more than one occasion when Harry will turn to his Dog brother for help.

3
HRH the Princess Royal and Captain Mark Phillips

HRH the Princess Royal
Birthdate: 15 August 1950
Born in the Year of the Tiger

Like her mother, the Princess Royal was born in the Year of the Tiger. But unlike the Queen, Anne's Tiger temperament has never been subjected to the rigors of responsibility that are the monarch's lot. Not that the Tiger can't handle responsibilities; quite the opposite. Tigers love to be the boss and the Chinese Horoscopes point out that it is a very unusual Tiger indeed who doesn't leap at an opportunity to run the show. But being the supreme chief—the general, the chairman, and in some cases the Queen—is a job Tigers neither enjoy fully nor are best suited for. Given the choice, Tigers, who are naturally rebellious prefer to front a small band. It is here that they feel the freedom to exercise their own special brand of dynamic leadership. Whereas Her Majesty the Queen is a Tiger whose natural sense of rebellion has, in a sense, been tamed, caged one could say, by her position as sovereign, the Princess Royal has no such restraints. As we shall see, Anne's Tiger sign has virtually dominated her life.

Early years

It can truthfully be said that Tigers are born with an unfair advantage, in that they have the major shareholding in vigour and no other sign seems to have such an endless stream of brilliant ideas on tap. But Tigers do have a serious flaw in their characters. Brilliant and dynamic they might be, but unless Tigers can dig deep into their personalities and discover the reality that lies within they quickly become depressed. This is why the Chinese Horoscopes class the Tiger sign as short-paced. It also accounts for the unpredictability that surrounds the Tiger at every level.

The year that Princess Anne was born bore all the hallmarks of the Tiger's sometimes dramatic changeability. Indeed, the whole of 1950 was coloured by the growing conflict in Korea. The very day Anne was born there was a severe earthquake in Assan. And the rebel side of the Tiger wasn't to be outdone. In China, after thousands of years, child marriages, sexual inequality, and polygamy were permanently outlawed.

In childhood, the sudden reversal of spirits which is an integral characteristic of the Tiger sign, is a common occurrence. Tiger children are prone to long periods of inner uncertainty which can cause major problems for both parents and siblings alike. Tiger kids are thought of as moody, stubborn and difficult, and for good reason. Tigers find it an up-hill task to rationalize their inner gloom, and for a Tiger child it is impossible. Happy one minute, cast down the next, this is the lot of the tiny Tiger.

Tigers are born to attack authority and Tiger children find that the heavy doses that usually surround childhood present a genuine obstacle to happiness. But an even greater obstacle is created when a Tiger's parents both have non-compatible signs. This was certainly true for Princess Anne. To begin with, her mother is also a Tiger. This is not good news. Two Tigers under the same roof are thought highly inauspicious by the Chinese Horoscopes. They score no marks at all for understanding. The same, unfortunately, is true of the relationship between herself and her Rooster father Philip. To make matters worse, the other members of Anne's close family, the Queen Mother and brother Charles were both born in a Rat year, a sign which is only a fraction better in terms of a relationship with a Tiger. It has been frequently stated that the young Tiger Princess was not her grandmother's favourite. And it still rankles that as number two (not a Tiger's most cherished position) Anne was made to stay at home while Charles went to their mother's Coronation. 'I was always in second place,' she once admitted with a touch of irony, 'a tail-end Charlie.'

However, in spite of the lack of understanding which is commonplace between two Tigers, a Tiger mother makes a first-rate parent. They teach by example and are never hypocritical. Rooster fathers are similar, although they tend to have a more conservative attitude towards discipline. Prince Philip, for example, once smacked Anne because she didn't put her jumper on as he had told her. But her father's heavy hand only served to activate the rebel in Anne's Tiger sign, to bring out the fierce competitor which lurks in the hearts of Tigers everywhere. With her elder brother as the man to beat, Anne pushed herself. When the Queen wasn't reading to her from the Bible (Tiger parents love to tell their offspring stories), Philip was teaching Anne to swim in the Palace pool. Before long she could outswim Charles. It was the same story when Anne learned to ride; she was off the leading rein long before her Rat brother. 'When we were children,' Anne recalls, 'we used to fight like cat and dog.' Had Anne known their Chinese animal signs, she would have surely said Tiger and Rat since Cats and Dogs get on surprisingly well.

When Charles went to boarding school, Anne was left to pace herself. Alone in the Palace, with only two well-bought-up little girls and her nurse, the aptly nicknamed 'No-Nonsense' Lightbody, Anne continued to assert herself and gave full vent to the rebellious side of her influencing sign. She said of that time: 'Up to my teens I don't think I went along with the family bit'. Classed as 'boisterous, bossy and moody' Anne was never at ease with the royal conventions which were shoved at her from all directions. In 1973, when the Tiger princess was just 23, Anne gave an interview in which she said something that could have been taken from any Chinese Horoscope handbook on the Tiger personality. 'I'm me, I'm a person,' she said, 'I'm an individual, and I think it's better for everybody that I am me and shouldn't try to pretend to be anything I'm not.'

Middle years

There are a number of animal signs which have an overlap of characteristics. Goats and Pigs, for example, both enjoy performing and take naturally to any enterprise which gives them a chance to show off. The Tiger and Dragon share a hot head and it would be difficult to pick which of the two signs has the shorter fuse. The middle period of a Tiger's life is considered the most dangerous and their well-being can hardly be made safer by an impetuous and highly explosive temperament. Bearing this in mind it is no wonder Anne was booked for driving her Reliant Scimitar GTE at an estimated 120 m.p.h. down the motorway. And there was a time not so long ago in which Princess Anne's Tiger tongue was found working overtime. Not a day went by without at least one member of the press getting it in the neck. Tigers simply cannot bear being pushed around. Once placed at the mercy of someone else's decision they react at once. Tigers, especially when they are young princesses want things done their way or not at all. Opposing views are seen as attempts to override the Tiger's authority and are dealt with instantly by a verbal slap in the face. During her early twenties, at a time when Anne was coming to terms with self-belief through her love of three-day eventing, her 'rudeness' became something of a legend. Indeed, there were enough to form an anthology. Here are a few:

> *To a photographer at a horse trial*: 'Don't you think I've got enough problems without you?'
> *To an Australian cameraman*: 'I'm not your love. I am your Royal Highness.'
> *To the press at the Badminton Horse Trials*: 'Why don't you just naff off?'

Most of the bad press Anne received for her least attractive of the Tiger's influences occurred during the period when Anne's life was almost exclusively devoted to horses. And because she was so much in the public eye, Anne naturally attracted more than her share of public curiosity. The press never left her alone. That Princess Anne was an outstanding rider is not in doubt, but it was a fact that became overshadowed by both her royal blood and her outspoken manner. In most cases Anne's outbursts were entirely justified. Horses are sensitive creatures, especially the show jumping breeds and a noisy click from a camera at a vital moment can be unsettling. It may sometimes lose the rider the contest. More importantly, the Chinese Horoscopes reveal that Tigers and Horses have one form of relationship in which they achieve maximum points. In business, Tigers and Horses have perfect understanding. It could be added that a successful rider and horse are in every sense a business partnership! Given this important, if slightly fanciful, insight, it is perhaps no wonder that Anne crowned a career of competitive riding by winning a place in the British team at the Montreal Olympics. What is more important still, in terms of the ever-present Tiger influence, is that Princess Anne more or less taught herself. 'I learned "eventing" myself,' she says, 'and everything I did, I did for myself.' At no time was Anne ever out of the top dozen female riders in Britain.

Good horsemanship also requires courage, which is another of the Tiger sign's great qualities. Tigers are, in fact, born under the sign of courage, and large doses of bravery are never more necessary than getting back in the saddle after falling of a fast-moving stallion. In 1965 Anne broke her nose, in 1973 she bruised her shoulder and thigh, and in 1976 she cracked a vertebra and was concussed. Each time the press caught the Tiger's full fury, but there was justification. As Anne points out, 'When you've fallen off your horse four times, you don't want to be asked what you had for breakfast'.

The future

In her late thirties, the Princess Royal is past her best as a competitive three-day eventer, but her work for Save the Children has more than compensated for any gap she might have felt. And her list of royal engagements almost doubles that of some of the other members of the Royal Family. Her annual figure for public engagements is in the region of 300 plus—a minimum of one for every working day. One journalist reported that at three o'clock she was the 137th person Princess Anne had met that day.

Charities like Save the Children now completely absorb Anne's attention and it is fundamental to the Tiger's nature to display great generosity. Although, like her Tiger mother, Anne confesses meanness with money—she once said, 'A good suit goes on for ever'—this in no way contradicts her animal influence. Her generosity, like the Queen's is through public patronage and giving 'herself', rather than just donating cash. And anyway, to be thrifty does not deny generosity. A quick mind, so typical of the Tiger, is a most valuable asset when raising the vast sums of money that charities the size of Save the Children require. In Australia, when Michael Parkinson asked her for a TV interview, she agreed if he paid £6,000 to the Save the Children Fund.

Again, the Tiger's influence is much in evidence whenever she adopts the role of fundraiser. Tigers have to be actively involved with the team, which is why they do their best work as captain of a small group rather than giving orders from the sidelines. The director of Home Farm Trust related that Princess Anne would only be a patron if she were allowed to become deeply involved with the charity's work. 'She made it plain,' he said, 'she didn't want to be just a figurehead.'

All who are close to Princess Anne agree that she has now come through the most difficult phase of her life. In having found fundraising, and charity work as a whole, a worthwhile cause, Anne has gone a long way to discovering the 'me' that the Tiger so desperately demands to recognize. Realizing this will release much of the inner tension Tigers feel when they are uncertain as to their true identity. But once the Tiger is fully grown, those under its influence will discover they have few allies among the animal signs. Those signs who are not compatible—and there are several—had better beware. The all-time enemies of Tigers are those born in a Buffalo year. This means Anne's relationship with her Buffalo sister-in-law, Diana will plumb new depths. The two Princesses live less than 20 miles apart, and it is an open secret that they hardly every meet socially. More significantly, neither Anne nor Mark were asked to be godparents to Diana's children, which perhaps, is just as well. The Chinese Horoscopes warn that in the long term the stolid Buffalo will wear out the short-paced Tiger. But with Anne rapidly becoming everyone's favourite, a worn-out Tiger Princess Royal is the last thing her ever-growing army of fans would want. Given the circumstances and Anne's present attitude towards her Buffalo sister-in-law, it is probably the last thing they'll get.

Captain Mark Phillips
Birthdate: 22 September 1948
Born in the Year of the Rat

Captain Mark Phillips is one of a growing number of Rats who make up the Royal Family. In keeping with his influencing sign, Mark Phillips moves quickly when the opportunity presents itself. Charles once called him 'Foggy', the joke being that, it is said, he thought Mark wet and thick. Charles may have got the applause for his own Rat-influenced wit, but for once the Prince's observation was well off the mark—no pun intended. Captain Phillips may be shy, he may only care about horses, he may be short (comparatively) of cash, but when the chance to marry a real live princess presented itself he jumped in with both feet. The truth is that Captain Mark Phillips is neither wet nor thick. He saw a good thing and took it. What's more he has the know-how to maintain life as a royal without letting it become the kind of nightmare that other commoners have experienced. Lord Snowdon, the Duchess of Windsor, and Princess Michael of Kent are all commoners who have at one time fallen short of both the public and the Royal Family's expectations, and suffered as a result. But, thanks to the influence of his Rat sign, Mark has had the good sense to keep his nose well out of the limelight. He might not be everyone's favourite, but he is no one's pet hate.

Early years

Mark Phillips's mother is a member of the Tiarks banking family and his father a director of Wall's meat products (pies and sausages). His early years, well-heeled by most standards, were none the less poor in comparison with those enjoyed by his in-laws. But, in keeping with his two Rat brothers-in-law, Mark quickly found that the services appealed to his influencing animal's love of service life.

With its regular three meals a day, chummy atmosphere, and easy-going routine, an officer's life is tailor-made for the Rat personality. In common with Anne, Mark showed a love of horses from an early age and, like her, distinguished himself in the saddle. To become a successful sportsman requires dedication, but it also needs a sense of joy. No one can dedicate themselves to hours of training, year in, year out, unless there is a level of pleasure involved. All Rats are born with an instinct for pleasure, which, when coupled with their spirit of opportunism, makes them formidable sportsmen. Mark could ride before he could walk and in 1972, he won an Olympic gold. It was his prowess as a horseman that attracted Anne to Mark. As a friend put it, 'He was one of the very few riders Anne could never actually beat'.

Middle years

The Rat's middle years are the most troublesome, often faced with problems created by their innate sensuality and lack of thrift.

As Mark Phillips is clearly aware, a commoner marrying a princess brings massive financial problems that only inherited wealth or a vast steady income can solve. Mark may well come into a six figure fortune one day, but at the moment he finds it difficult making ends meet. The money that his wife receives from the Civil List nowhere near covers the huge expenses created by Gatcombe Park, the farm and estate given to them by the Queen when they married. To deal with his cash-flow problem, Mark did sponsorship deals with British Leyland and Daks menswear before the Palace let it be known that it was not acceptable to have such close links with commercialism. At one stage he collaborated on a book on equestrianism with TV presenter Angela Rippon. The relationship received a great deal of press rumour, and it has to be said that Ms Rippon, born in the Year of the Monkey (1944) has an influencing sign which cannot resist intrigue. What is more, Rats find it impossible to say no to their sensual urges. But Monkeys and Rats only have a fifty-fifty chance of any kind of successful relationship. Should they engage in an affair it will be fast and furious, with the Rat being the faster and more furious of the two. Remember Koo Stark and Andy? That was another Monkey and Rat relationship which followed the accepted pattern. Whatever the truth behind Angela Rippon and Mark Phillips, the former newsreader not only wrote a book about him, but got close enough to have the following insight. She said 'He's reserved and quiet until he knows people and then he's friendly with a good sense of humour'. Indeed, a sense of humour is vital when being constantly the object of media attention.

Fortunately, Rats are frequently saved by their sharp wits. In 1974, Anne was the victim of an armed kidnap attempt (the courage she displayed in that situation is another outstanding example of a characteristic of Anne's Tiger sign); the Phillipses were expected at an old friend's home for dinner and when Mark called to say he would be late, his friend asked 'Have you been held up?' There was a pause. Mark replied off the cuff 'Well you could say that'.

The future

Without large sums of money to sustain him and his family, Captain Mark Phillips must bide his time and continue farming, the least attractive of all jobs for a Rat—remember that rats raid farms for the grain in the barns, they don't actually grow it! And he has learned the fact that no one can be a royal one day and up to his neck in cow pats the next. Not even Charles has managed to convince the world at large that he is a serious farmer. No amount of pictures of him standing in the windswept Scottish Highlands suggests that Charles is any more than a royal town dweller doing a bit of weekend gardening. Mark, on the other hand, has got his image just right, that of a serious full-time farmer at one with the pigs and the silos.

As with Rats everywhere, Mark Phillips is a warm-hearted individual with an eye for the main chance. His big break was marrying Princess Anne but, whatever the future holds, Mark Phillips will have to remember to keep the undercurrent of aggression that all Rats tend to suffer from firmly in check. He certainly will not want a repeat performance of the time in Australia when he and his horsey entourage caused $8,000 dollars' worth of damage to their hotel.

Princess Anne and Captain Mark Phillips as marriage partners

The Chinese Horoscopes describe Tigers as impulsive creatures who risk all for love. Anne fell for Mark and although as a Rat he took the chance when it was offered, there is no doubt that Anne did a great deal of offering. But the romance was based in a dream world of horse riding, with the Tiger, at least, not thinking much about the future. As she said at the time prior to her engagement: 'He's very, very strong. Horses rarely stop with him, and if they do they wish they hadn't—but he's also sympathetic to different types of horses, which I think is rare in a man.'

Given the wide choice of partners, in theory at least, it seems extraordinary that Princess Anne married someone born in a Rat year. Tigers and Rats have nothing in common. Apart from a few sparks that invariably occur when strong members of opposite signs come into contact, love between Rat and Tiger is as rare as finding a second-hand car with a genuine low mileage. And on the subject of cars, both have been up before the beak on charges of speeding. In Anne's case, her law-breaking is largely due to her Tiger's rejection of authority—Tigers do what they want, when they want. Mark, on the other hand, drives fast because Rats love speed—it excites their powerful senses. In 1985, he was accused of reckless driving and in 1987, a Cat year (unfavourable for both Rats and Tigers), Mark narrowly avoided having his licence taken away and now has seven penalty points on his licence. Judging by these events, and in keeping with his animal sign's character, it is unlikely it will be his last trip to the magistrates court. And given his wife's love of fast cars, it might prove an alternative meeting place for the Princess Royal and her husband.

Not surprisingly, Anne and Mark Phillips are not seen in public very often. If there is a saving grace for a Tiger and a Rat, it might be found in the Rat's warmth and sense of humour. Tigers frequently endure periods where they simply cannot face the world. When their inner personality defies identification, the Tiger quickly slumps into a despondent heap. Anne is no exception. A friend of Princess Anne once described her as having 'a mercurial temperament'. The friend goes on to prove what the Chinese say: 'Some days are good and some days she's low spirited. Captain Phillips is good for her because he stops her brooding when things go wrong. He laughs her out of it.'

It could be argued that the kind of courage needed to keep an unhappy marriage together is different to the kind of courage it requires to watch a baby die of starvation, or reach out a hand to the severely mentally handicapped. But courage is something we have or haven't got, and facing domestic despair can be just as punishing as being a witness to the starving. As a Tiger, Princess Anne has courage in abundance. In her work for the Save the Children Fund and charities for the disabled, Anne uses her Tiger gift of courage to the full. When others step back, Anne steps forward. But bearing in mind the Tiger is short-paced, there is always a question mark as to how long it will be before the Tiger runs out of steam.

Princess Anne and Captain Mark Phillips as parents

If the Phillipses have a genuine bond outside a love of horses, it is their children. Although the Queen once remarked, 'I shouldn't wonder if their children are four-legged', Tigers and Rats, in their different ways, make excellent parents. Tigers lead by example and are great story-tellers. Although Rats tend to be fretful about their offspring, they have a genuine rapport. The problem is making sure that the differences which divide Tiger and Rat parents are not allowed to intrude too far into their children's world. More important still, Rats and Tigers must work out between them what kind of education their children are to have and stick to it. So often, when two signs have such starkly contrasting views, their children end up with a poor mix of the two. So far, the Tiger influence of the Princess Royal seems to have the upper hand. Having been so much under the public gaze herself, Anne has opted for complete secrecy for Peter and Zara. In fact, she goes out of her way to protect son and daughter from even the faintest public curiosity. When asked if she had to choose between her royal duties and her children, Anne responded in typical Tigerish fashion. 'I would choose my children,' she said without hesitation, and added, 'They have to be given the chance to grow up in reasonable normality. You don't want them to be landed with labels now, because one's conscious of the fact that everything will be discussed endlessly and remem-

The Rat is eager for new experiences

Buffalo ladies really go to town when the need arises

Pigs and Buffaloes get four out of five stars for friendship

The Rat and Buffalo are chalk and cheese—the heady days of new love frequently promise more than they can deliver

Dogs make first-rate leaders

It is fundamental to the Tiger's nature to display great generosity

Jason Fraser/SIPA, Rex Features Limited   Rex Features Limited

Shooting is an ideal way for male Rats to rid themselves of their aggression

An essential characteristic of the Pig personality—a love of dressing up and putting on a show

Bernard Morton, Camera Press London

Fox/The Keystone Collection

Dragons rely on self-assurance—I love me, why don't you?

Tigers and Pigs score almost top points for compatibility

Tigers know their own mind and are not easily dissuaded

Roosters cannot resist getting into a uniform whenever the chance presents itself

Rex Features Limited   *The Keystone Collection*

Horse women in particular have wonderfully witty minds and bags of style

Buffaloes are complex animals and they are driven by an inner compulsion that is seldom, if ever, fully under control

Rats adore sweets things

The Horse and the Monkey score no marks for compatibility

The Pig is one sign to whom the Rooster will respond

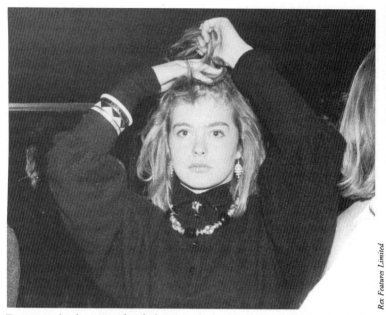

Dragons don't get to lead the parade by passing exams but by being noticed

Music gives the Rat and Dragon great pleasure

Cats are deeply sensuous

A curious feature of Snake women is a love of accessories. Female Snakes would rather die than be seen looking drab

No other animal enjoys dressing up with such relish or does so with such effect than the Pig

bered when they are older. They ought to be judged for themselves when they get older.'

Peter Phillips
Birthdate: 15 November 1977
Born in the Year of the Snake
Zara Phillips
Birthdate: 15 May 1981
Born in the Year of the Rooster

Neither child has a title and, like their father Mark, both are commoners. But because of their mother's almost obsessive desire for privacy for her two young children there is very little in the way of information about their lives. Fortunately, the Chinese Horoscopes alter that. We know, for example, that Peter Phillips having a Snake as his governing influence will be slow to develop. This in itself is one of the most significant factors governing a Snake's early years. However, it is certain that Peter Phillips will inherit artistic gifts, probably musical, and have a strong appreciation of beauty. Unless, like Gandhi, there is a religious quality attached to leadership, Snakes usually make poor leaders. They are indecisive when pressed and Snakes are not generous with money, a fact which young Peter's school friends may have already discovered when buying jam buns at the tuck shop. Possessive to a marked degree, Snakes in love cannot let go the object of their deep-running passion. The Chinese also say that female Snakes have the power to bewitch and male Snakes have a subtle sense of humour. But the fact that Snakes take ages to mature will eventually send Peter Phillips's action-packed Tiger mother round the bend, or at least shed a stripe or two. And, for once, Daddy Rat will be in total agreement. 'What's wrong with the boy?' Rat and Tiger parent will be asking each other, almost daily. The answer will be, of course, that Master Phillips is simply acting under the influence of his Snake sign. Incidently, royal Snakes are very thin on the ground. The only monarchs born in a Snake year were Anne and Elizabeth I.

By contrast, Zara's personality will be entirely familiar to Anne, since she is the same sign as Anne's own father. Usually spend-thrift but methodical, Roosters are quick to learn and are out-spoken to a fault. Her life will be governed by a candid attitude to most things and there will be little deviation from accepted modes of behaviour. Zara will love to garden, organize those around her, and keep her ideas and thoughts written down. Lacking initiative, the young Rooster will nevertheless be a happy child, if a little over-critical of those with less conservative views. As she grows older, Zara will not be having fun behind the bike shed—sexual freedom is *not* on the Rooster's syllabus.

Unhappily for Mark Phillips, he has no understanding of Rooster Zara, but he does have a little more in common with his Snake son. And poor Princess Anne could not have got it more wrong. She has zero compatibility with her Rooster daughter and Rooster father, zero with her Tiger mother, zero with her Rat husband, Rat brothers and Rat grandmother, zero with her Buffalo sister-in-law and just one star out of five for compatibility with her Snake son. No wonder she's a touchy Tiger.

4
The Duke and Duchess of York

The Duke of York
Birthdate: 19 February 1960
Born in the Year of the Rat

The overwhelming majority of those born in the Rat year are free-wheelers; easy-going folk who take life as it comes. They have a love of all things sensual and enjoy a keen and often perceptive sense of humour. But there are a handful of Rats who let their undercurrent of aggression get the better of them. Here, the fun-loving Rat becomes obsessed with trivial details and maps out life in painstaking detail. Neither Andrew nor his Rat brother Charles display the extreme characteristics of their influencing sign, although it has to be said that when two Rats live under the same roof one is usually forced into a position of taking on the 'responsible' role. The elder brother, in this case, does show the odd touch of the introvert Rat. His speech patterns, for example, contain several repressed features and his body language is never entirely comfortable. But the Chinese Horoscopes would point out that Charles is far from being a repressed Rat—the planner and petty authoritarian. As heir to the throne, Charles simply has been forced at times to keep his influencing animal sign more or less in check, while Andrew, unconcerned with the responsibilities that surround a future monarch, is free to explore his Rat's influence to the outer limits. And this he does, it would seem, at every available opportunity. From what we have seen from his behaviour so far, Prince Andrew has his full share of the Rat's influence. More than any other sign, the Rat cannot wait to get on with life. Rats are ruled by their senses and quick wits and whatever they do, they do it to the full.

Early years

The spirit of opportunism is a pronounced feature of the Rat year, with a heavy emphasis on financial matters. The year that the Duke of York was born showed all the Rat traits. In March, new pound notes were issued and in December, the worthless farthing ceased to be legal tender. But the Chinese warn that Rats are not normally cut out for dreary routine work and their year will always experience a few hiccups, some serious. Four days after Andrew was born, Agadir was destroyed by an earthquake.

In the Chinese Horoscopes, in addition to the year influencing our behaviour, the month, week, day, and hour (each with its own animal sign) all have a modifying effect on the yearly animal sign. It is the combination of these modifying signs that give people their degree of individuality. But it must be stressed that the yearly sign is by far the strongest influence. Most people who consult me about their animal signs seldom, if ever have such information to hand. Few know what time they were born, and, although it is easy to work out, the actual day of our birth is not something we usually have to hand. But I mention it here because the Duke of York's hour of birth is publicly recorded and often given in books about him: it was 3:30 in the afternoon—the hour of the Monkey. Hours in China are the length of two Western hours. The first hour of the animal cycle of hours is 11 p.m. to 1 a.m., and is governed by the Rat. Then, as with the yearly signs, the remaining 11 animals follow in sequence. The Chinese point out that Rats born in a Monkey hour have few scruples. Furthermore, they say that to the Rat's pronounced charm and opportunism is added a highly developed sense of trickery. This is certainly true of

Andrew. From a very early age, the young Prince could not resist monkeying around. He relished thinking up practical jokes and his schooldays provided an ample opportunity to perform them.

In 1968, the Duke of York went to Gordonstoun, as did his father and two brothers. 'He loved making apple pie beds,' an old school chum recalls, 'but always felt badly if it got out of hand.' One such joke involved the German ambassador and his wife during their visit to the school's big night, the annual Feast of Agar. While the distinguished guests were eating, Andrew nipped into their room and covered the loo with cling film. Another favourite trick at Gordonstoun involved phoning distant royals like his cousin Juan Carlos of Spain. Disguising his voice, Andrew would say that he'd like to leave a message for Dick Head. He'd do this half a dozen times. After an hour or so he'd ring up and say he was Dick Head, and ask if there were any messages.

Teachers often point out that their classes show a marked difference from one year to the next, which in my view substantiates the claims made by Chinese Horoscopes that each year is influenced by one of the 12 animal signs. To add fuel to the argument, many note that classes duplicate themselves in terms of both behaviour and achievements every 12 years—another illustration of the Chinese animal signs at work. Andrew and Charles are 12 years apart in age and their sign had a similar influence over both of them during their days at Gordonstoun. The two Princes enjoyed the challenge of outdoor life and threw themselves into each new experience with typical Rat-like enthusiasm. But of the two Rat brothers, Andrew seems to have enjoyed his time there the most. He excelled at games and always opted for the school's outdoor activities—much being made of the fact that Gordonstoun had just received its first intake of 30 girls. And although his Tiger mother complained that her son watched too much television and his Rooster father considered Andrew's clothes 'somewhat brash', the student Prince passed six O levels and three A levels.

But it wasn't Andrew's educational prowess which caught the

imagination of both press and public alike. When Andrew went to Canada to spend two terms at Lakefield College, Ontario, he was greeted like a pop star by teenage girls. It was the girls of Lakefield College who dubbed him with the nickname of 'Randy Andy' and it was with good reason that Charles called his younger brother 'the one with the Robert Redford looks'. With his Rat's charm simply oozing out in all directions it is no wonder that girls quite literally threw themselves at the Prince. They threw themselves at Charles, of course—some topless, as we recall—but the Prince of Wales's response has always been more diffident. But without the constantly nagging thought that he is heir to the throne and must act accordingly, Andrew has been able to indulge himself as only a Rat is able. As he once explained: 'Because I haven't been the centre of attention, I have been able to lead my own life'. In Canada, whenever the Prince hoved into view, young girls screamed 'We want Andy'. In the case of Sandi Jones, born in the same Rat year as Andrew, the request was granted. Sandi was the first in Andy's long list of conquests, which also included Kirsty Richmond. Born in the year of the Pig, the same sign as the Duchess of York, the young Canadian was deeply affected by Andrew's charm. She wasn't the only young woman to be bowled over by Andy's line of chat, which was measured at the time by one of Kirsty's friends, who made the somewhat loaded comment 'It was just Kirsty's turn'. A less loaded, but equally astute, view of the Rat's charm-dispensing influence at that time comes from Julia Guinness, the younger sister of Charles's ex, Sabrina: 'He's a bit of a flirt,' she says, 'but the most charming person you could hope to meet'.

The Chinese Horoscopes point out that the Rat will often prefer to live off their wits rather than put in hours of physical toil. Most Rats prefer life when all the dull incidentals are taken care of. Rats are usually not bothered by keeping up to date with fashion and, providing the sweet-trolly is groaning, trendy cuisine does not feature greatly in their scheme of things. Lots and often is the Rat's standard attitude to food. Given the armed services' insistence on a well-stocked provisions tent, the Army, Navy, and

Air Force would seem to have been designed almost exclusively for the Rat personality. Clothes and provisions are handed out at no cost and, although the routine may prove tedious for some, sharp-minded, opportunist Rats will always find a way to use the system to suit themselves. In the Navy, free and constant travel is a central attraction for the Rat—many of whom take naturally to water. Aged 19, and without very clear ideas as to his future, Andrew let family tradition, and not a little of the Rat's influence, take the tiller. In 1979, he joined the Royal Navy as a trainee helicopter pilot.

There are, however, a few dodgy moments for a sailor, even in 'peace' time. The war in the Falklands was one such period for Andrew. The Rat is no coward and the undercurrent of aggression that is to be found in all Rats was given full chance to express itself during this painful, and some say unnecessary, conflict. Even so, Andrew found staring death in the face a less than stimulating experience. 'I have been frightened,' he admitted with typical Rat subjectivity, 'If I had the choice, I would not want to go through it again.'

Middle years

Although still in his twenties, the Duke of York has, by virtue of his experiences in the South Atlantic, grown into manhood. Those who know him say that he entered the Falklands War a child and came home a man. It was on his return that he became seriously involved with Koo Stark, who he had met just before the Task Force sailed. Andrew had met Koo at Tramps, a fashionable night club in London, and the couple kept in close touch throughout Andrew's service in the Falklands.

Of the many women who have helped substantiate the 'Randy Andy' tag, Koo unquestionably held the greatest sway. She got closer than anyone, apart from his bride Sarah, to understanding the more sensitive side to Andrew's nature. In this, Koo was helped enormously by her animal sign. She was born on 26 April 1956, the Year of the Monkey. Although only four years older,

Koo was considerably more mature than Andrew at the time of their meeting. Now a serious photographer, as well as an actress, Koo is every inch the classic Monkey lady. I met her first when she appeared on my Radio Four Programme on Chinese Horoscopes and I was struck at once by her overwhelming self-possession, a quality which the sensuous, fast-moving Rat would find utterly irresistible. Her hair is thick and falls naturally while her complexion is smooth and prone to blushing—exactly as the Chinese Horoscopes explain. But Koo's most seductive feature is to be found in her eyes. They have all the sparkle of a cut diamond, and much of a gem's icy coolness. I can honestly say I have never seen eyes like Koo Stark's and it is easy to see how Andrew fell for the young Monkey. What's more, Koo's influencing sign has dished her out an extra strong helping of wickedly quick wits which, combined with an adaptable sense of humour and a keen intellect, makes the attraction for the Rat pretty well fatal.

The Chinese Horoscopes give a Rat and a Monkey in love, four out of five stars for compatibility. The sensuous, witty Rat and the wise yet sometimes crafty Monkey are ideal partners in the conspiratorial aspects of being in love, enhanced when one of the partners is third in line to the throne and the other is known mainly for appearing in soft porn films. As one would expect from two signs so adept at outwitting the field, Andrew and Koo did an excellent job during their brief encounter. This conspiratorial side was especially evident when they flew off to Princess Margaret's holiday home in the paradise island of Mustique. With the press and photographers being reduced to walking (taxis were told to refuse to carry newsmen) Andy and Koo were free to drive around in their Land Rover with comparative ease. The couple even boarded the plane under the names of Mr and Mrs Cambridge.

On his return to England, Andrew sadly discovered that Koo was not the bride his parents wanted for him. Neither his Tiger mother nor his Rooster father have much time for Monkeys. The Rooster is critical of the Monkey's love of intrigue and the Tiger suspicious of their sometimes all too effortless adaptability. However, the bride that Andrew chose was more auspicious in terms of the Chinese scale of animal compatibility, both in terms of his own and his parents's signs. Whereas Rat and Monkey get four out of five stars when in love, the relationship drops a star when they marry. For a Pig—Sarah's sign—and a Rat, the process is reversed and a Pig and a Rat get near full marks when marrying. What's more, Pig daughters-in-law and Tiger mothers-in-law get along really well!

If Andrew had married Koo, he would have added a third Monkey to a list of women who have made their mark on the Royal Family in circumstances that have not always met with total royal approval. The late Duchess of Windsor was born in a Monkey year (1896), as was Princess Michael of Kent (15 January 1945). Without being unkind, I think it would be fair to say that both women have not enjoyed the unrestrained enthusiasm that British subjects usually reserve for even the fringe members of royalty. For Koo's sake, if not Andrew's, it may have been just as well that their love blossomed in the Year of the Dog, whose idealism stands firm against even a slight false note.

Through Koo, Andrew learned photography and was able to give vent to the artistic side of his Rat's influence. Within a short time, Andrew quickly acquired no less than five cameras—so like the eager Rat—which includes his mother's marvellous Hasselblad, given to the Queen on a state visit to Sweden. Although largely undistinguished, his work so far has the quality of enthusiasm, which is both positive and promising. Whether he will continue to explore this demanding craft remains to be seen, but to do so without someone to share in its progress would be unusual for a Rat. But Rats are tenacious when the need arises. As with all things, a Rat's tenacity can only be measured by the desirability of the object in question. And should Andrew tire of shooting with his cameras, he can easily turn to a pair of magnificent Purdey shotguns, given to him by Charles when he first began flirting with vegetarianism. Shooting is an ideal way for male Rats to rid themselves of their aggression. So is disco dancing, canoeing, and playing practical jokes—all of which seem central features of Andrew's early to middle years.

The future

Having tasted the Navy's agreeable social life, it is entirely understandable that Andrew should want it to be his career. As an officer in the senior service, his life is just about as comfortable as any Rat could wish. The feeling is, however, that he will one day be asked to take on a more public role and extend his portfolio of patronages. This will no doubt happen now Andrew and Sarah have begun a family.

The Duchess of York
Birthdate: 15 October 1959
Born in the Year of the Pig

There are two pronounced features of the Pig character that set them apart from the 11 other animal signs. The Pig has an enormous capacity to work hard and play hard. They can burn the candle at both ends and the middle, 24 hours a day, eight days a week. And no one is more sociable or better suited to form partnerships. Pigs have a flair for both enjoying life, which they do with a robust good will, and making long-lasting friendships. To find a miserable solitary soul born under the Pig's influence is as unusual as seeing one flying. These two main features of the Pig's influence summarize the Duchess of York. Breezy and full of go, she is the extravert female Pig from the tip of her noticeable red hair to the heels of her flying boots.

Early years

The year in which Fergie was born, 1959, did not provide outstanding examples of the Pig's influence. But there were enough events to distinguish it from the more anxious, well-meaning Dog year that preceded it. In spite of the pigsty image created by Western culture, Pigs are terribly clean animals. In July, the Litter Act was passed, which made it an offence to drop litter, and August saw the Street Offences Act come into force. Essentially a conservative animal, it could be argued that Pigs might easily favour the Conservative Party. This was undoubtably the case in October 1959. Seven days before Sarah Ferguson was born, the Tories were returned with a majority of 100 seats.

The Chinese point out that Pigs usually enjoy an uncomplicated and well-balanced childhood. Sarah certainly experienced no serious problems in her very young days. She frequently played with her future husband on the polo grounds at Windsor, where her father, Major Ronald Ferguson spent a great deal of time. Uncomplicated and well-meaning, Pigs will always do their best for others, especially Dogs. Those born under the signs of both Pig and Dog have a splendid understanding and rate highly on the compatibility scale. This may also explain why the 6-year-old Fergie, while out riding on her father's estate, once plunged into the River Test to save a mongrel puppy from drowning. By the way, neither Fergie nor the puppy could swim.

At school, Sarah worked hard but did not overdo it. Pigs are naturally bright, if a little easily duped at times, and the Duchess left her school, Hurst Lodge in Berkshire, with six O levels and her name on the board of headgirls. It was at her boarding school that Sarah displayed two essential characteristics of the Pig personality—a love of dressing up and putting on a show, and an appetite for generous helpings of food of any kind. At Hurst Lodge, Sarah earned the nickname 'Seconds' for raiding the school pantry and organizing midnight feasts.

But the contentment of her early childhood quickly turned sour, when her mother Susan left her father to marry the Argentine polo player, Hector Barrantes. It was a serious blow to Sarah's self-confidence, but one which the big-hearted influence of her Pig sign was more than capable of dealing with. And, fortunately for Sarah, her father's sign has had much to do with her recovery and continuing self-assurance. Major Ferguson was born in 1931, the Year of the Goat. Parents born in a Goat year have a four out of five star understanding of their Pig offspring and express their concern through a thorough coaching in the social graces. First-class manners, good food and wine, and dressing to suit the occasion are all qualities an attentive Goat father will instill in his Pig child. There can be no denying that Fergie loves dress balls, eating well, and lively dinner parties. Her gushing manners, however, I believe will improve with the advent of motherhood, a period when Fergie could be forced to take a more inwardly reflective position than she has hitherto.

In some way, Sarah's mother leaving her and sister Jane was not without its redeeming feature, painful though it must have been at the time. Major Ferguson's first wife was born in the Year of the Buffalo (1937) a sign that has little or no understanding of the infant Pig. Instead of light-hearted encouragement Buffaloes demand a great deal from their children in terms of obedience and place a heavy emphasis on discipline. Yet, whereas Pigs and Buffaloes get no stars at all on the scale of compatibility for a parent and child relationship, they score five out of five for friendship. Princess Diana, remember, is a Buffalo, and it is clear to everyone except a few Fleet Street royal watchers starved of a sensational story that the Princess and Duchess have an exceptional understanding.

Middle years

Facing her early thirties, the Duchess of York is already adjusting well to her life in the intimate circle of the Royal Family, and there can be no question that in time she will emerge as a strong and supportive member. She has, of course, had a great deal more experience of life than would normally be expected from a young woman in her position, and much has to do with her influencing sign. For example, Pigs adore work, and show an even greater aptitude for it if there's fun to be had into the bargain. Love of clothes, society and food again were a feature of her string of jobs before remeeting Andrew. Fergie worked as a shop assistant in Harrods' ski department, a courier for a firm of travel agents, a waitress in a fashionable Chelsea restaurant, a driver for a firm who cooked director's lunches, and a chalet girl in the trendy ski resorts of Gstaad and Murren. At all times, Sarah's animal sign, the industrious and fun-loving Pig was never absent for a minute. A flat-mate of that time, Suki Portman says of Sarah; 'She was incredibly industrious. She'd be up to all hours at some charity bash, then behind the counter or whatever in the morning.' Another example of the Pig's bright and shiny view of life is presented by Fergie's former boss, PR man Peter Cunard. He said, 'She was always jolly—never bitchy. If I, or anyone else in the office, felt a bit low, you could always go and have a word with her and you'd soon be cheered up.'

An early benefactor of Sarah's obvious cheerfulness, not to mention her strong physical self-awareness, was her first serious romantic partner, Kim Smith-Bingham. Like her father-in-law, Smith-Bingham was born in the Year of the Rooster. He said of the time they spent together, 'Sarah is a marvellous hostess. People say that red-heads have a terrible temper. Sarah didn't.' Always keen to stand out in a gathering, male Roosters and female Pigs will be great fun at any social event. A Rooster and a Pig have a better than average romance but marriage is not advised. Clearly both Kim and Sarah realized marriage was never on the cards. As Bingham said after the affair, 'We were both too ambitious and busy to settle down. We just drifted apart . . .'

An even temper is consistent with the Pig personality and so is their indifference towards insults and gossip about them. Pigs generally care little for their reputation and their view is linked to having a high opinion of their worth. Most Pigs know their own value to the very last percentage point, but when they fall in love, Pigs do so heavily and tend to wear their hearts on their sleeves. They might even become boastful, showing off their new lovers as if he or she were an Ascot hat.

Sarah Ferguson made no effort to conceal her relationship with either Kim Smith-Bingham or the man she left him for, the fast-living racing manager Paddy McNally. The honest Pig is a poor liar and it does most Pigs credit that they seldom bother trying. When Sarah went to live with McNally, everyone in her family knew. McNally is a Buffalo (born 1937) and presents another highly compatible sign for the Pig. But although Sarah was eager to marry McNally, the Buffalo, as ever, wasn't to be pushed. Three years after their meeting, Sarah flew back from Paddy McNally's Geneva home and rented a flat in the now fashionable London suburb of Clapham. In 1985, the Year of the Buffalo, a time when there is little room for deceit but plenty of space for family life to grow secure and strong, Sarah once again met Prince Andrew, her childhood friend from the lawns at Windsor. It would seem that the Rat and Pig, having explored other partners finally decided that the auspiciousness of their signs could not be ignored.

The future

Future happiness for many depends largely on the comfort they derive from making plans. Even if they don't always work out, making a plan provides some kind of notion that we are not entirely at the mercy of fate. Pigs, though, are not great planners. All too often they embark on a course of action when it is clear to everyone else that the time to act is long past. Pigs either act too early or too late. Finding the right moment is almost impossible for the Pig personality. In many ways, this has been true of the Duchess of York. The very nature of her romance with Andrew, his proposal of marriage and her acceptance of it all happened in an unplanned, some would say entirely spontaneous rush. But then that is what we would expect from a Rat and Pig partnership. Both animals follow their impulses, suggesting a future as one of instant decisions with a leaning towards fun and self-interest, which paradoxically in the case of the Pig nearly always involves the interest of others. Few other animal signs care so strongly for the well-being of those around them, or do so much to provide for it.

Not, as a rule, given to great introspection, Pigs prefer company to long hours sitting alone. Much of Fergie's future life will be spent in the close circle of her new family and she is fortunate to a marked degree that most of her in-laws have extremely compatible signs. Her mother-in-law is a Tiger and the Chinese Horoscopes point out that Tigers and Pigs score almost top points for compatibility and are capable of forming firm, good-humoured, and lasting friendships. This means Sarah will also form a positive relationship with Princess Anne, another Tiger. An understanding is on the cards with Captain Mark Phillips, who is a Rat like Fergie's husband and her brother-in-law Charles. The Buffalo Diana gets a four out of five star rating for friendship with Pig Fergie, while Philip the Rooster is awarded only one star less. Edward is a Dragon, and here again the rating is auspicious—three stars. However, it is said that Princess Margaret and the Duke and Duchess of York get on well, but the Chinese Horoscopes disagree. They warn that Princess Margaret (a Horse born in 1930) has an unpredictable animal sign when it comes to forming long-term friendships. For no apparent reason Horses may quickly grow bored, and friends as well as business associates, husbands, wives all suffer as a result. The point is that Horses must be free to exercise their independence and it follows that any friend who gets too close might well be seen to be a potential rider on their back.

The Chinese Horoscopes warn that the middle years of a Pig's life can sometimes get messy—the result of poor housekeeping and a too easily influenced heart. But those who weather these difficult times will find in old age that life gets better all the time. The Duchess of York has taken pains to ensure her middle years, if not exactly planned, are well provided for. Because of her Pig's influence, Sarah is not much concerned with putting on a front. True, she adores the side of her Pig nature which can't resist dressing up (remember that awful flying outfit she wore the day she got her private pilot's licence?) but her face is human, open, and, above all, honest. All these qualities are admired by the no-nonsense Rooster and held in high esteem by the dutiful

Tiger. As well as a mother, the Duchess of York's role, therefore, will be one of a highly amusing daughter-in-law and a fun-loving sailor's wife who makes his leave something really worth coming ashore for.

The Duke and Duchess of York as marriage partners

Given the wide choice of marriage partners facing the sons and daughter of Her Majesty the Queen, it is surprising that only Andrew has married in accordance with the Chinese Horoscopes. Rat and Pig get four from a maximum of five stars, which suggests a long and happy partnership. As long as Andrew can be free to express his joy of life as generated by his Rat sign and Sarah can indulge her Pig's natural flair for fun, there will be very little to stand in the way of the Yorks being the most solid and dependable marriage of all the Queen's children's. In times of strife, should there be any, it will be Fergie who'll do the repair work. The Pig's influence, it should be underlined is never more powerful than when attempting to build a bridge over troubled waters.

The Duke and Duchess of York as parents

Sarah will be a perfect mother. Happy in their home, a Pig mum will always ensure that her piglets are well fed, well informed and well behaved. Although they take a genuine interest in the finer points of their children's education, Rat fathers tend to fret over their children. Pigs, however, have a calming influence which will benefit both child and fellow parent alike. Andrew says, 'When we have a son, I'd like him to have an entirely normal life just like me'. He was, of course, using the word 'normal' in a royal context.

Princess Beatrice Elizabeth Mary of York

Birthdate: 8 August 1988
Born in the Year of the Dragon

It must be said that a baby Dragon in the York's home is just about perfect. Rat fathers dote on a Dragon child and as they grow older, the Dragon will provide stimulating company for both dad and mum. When *The Times* headline on the day the little Dragon girl was born read, 'At 8.18 on 8.8.88—a safe and lucky Royal birth', they were nearer the truth than their stab at numerology suggested. Dragons are indeed lucky, born under the sign of luck. This new arrival now means there are seven Dragons in the House of Windsor, beating the number of royal Rats by one.

5
Prince Edward

Prince Edward
Birthdate: 10 March 1964
Born in the Year of the Dragon

Since, in China, Dragons are the carnival kings it might one
day be regretted that the Queen didn't have her children in
reverse order. If Edward had been the first and not the last of her
sons, he would have found the job of sovereign a perfect match for
his Dragon sign. In China, moreover, there would have been no
question of a Rat like Charles, or Andrew, becoming King. If
there's a Dragon around, the job is theirs. Dragons achieve their
popularity in spite of a terrible temper, having no sense of
diplomacy, and lacking any sense of emotional or political balance. Dragons succeed for one clearly identifiable characteristic.
Dragons succeed because they love to be loved.

The Dragon sign is masculine in the extreme, and male
Dragons are noted for their mastery of winning others over by
sheer self-belief. So far, Prince Edward has displayed more than
a little of the Dragon's emphatic and instantly recognizable
personality and as he continues to emerge from the shadow cast
by the popularity of his brothers and sister there is every reason to
believe he will give full vent to his governing sign's many and
varied traits. Edward's quick temper has already been seen

regularly and, since no Dragon likes to be made fun of, there's a chance that we'll see it a good deal more.

Early years

1964, the year Edward was born carried with it many of the Dragon's most pronounced features. Dragon years are always unpredictable, but it is said that they start and finish with a major event, which may sometimes be symbolic of the razzle-dazzle associated with the Chinese New Year celebrations. As 1964 began, fierce fighting broke out between Greeks and Turks in Cyprus, while in December Donald Campbell broke the world water speed record.

In the last couple of years, Prince Edward has moved nearer the centre of the royal stage, winning as many friends as critics en route. Even so, it requires a nudge of the memory to recall a time when Edward was little more than a distant, somewhat shadowy figure to the public at large. Cruel and unfounded rumours about his dim wits were, sadly, plentiful. But they only served to illustrate a classic feature of the Dragon's early years. The Chinese say that young Dragons are terribly misunderstood. Although Dragon children have rich and powerful imaginations, they tend to be loners who strive for an inner perfection, which, because their personalities are as yet unformed, can be only partly realized. This may cause stress and frustration, but when self-belief and perfection are realized to the full we are then greeted with the phenomenon of the child prodigy. Among a long list of child prodigies are Shirley Temple, Salvador Dali, Bonnie Langford, and Yehudi Menuhin, all born in the Year of the Dragon. And not long ago, I read of an 11-year-old Chinese painter called Wang Yani, who had already completed over 4,000 beautiful paintings. However, for most Dragons, Prince Edward included, childhood is a long and unhappy period in which those around them simply do not understand their need for freedom. Some signs prefer the safety net provided by rules and regulations. But not the Dragon.

In spite of the fact that as a Dragon child, he was probably often on his own and misunderstood, Edward did enjoy some advantages over his Rat brothers and Tiger sister. Whereas Tigers and Rats have little or no understanding, Dragons are loved by the Rat and admired by the Tiger. This also means that Edward is his Tiger mother's most auspicious offspring. And it gets better. The Dragon Edward also has his Rooster father's full approval—something neither his Rat nor Tiger siblings experienced. According to the ever-perceptive Chinese Horoscopes, until Edward came along, family get-togethers at Buck House were dismally inauspicious occasions. No wonder the young Prince Edward, sensing the lack of communication around him, told Neil Armstrong, 'My ambition is to be an astronaut'. Obviously the moon seemed just about far enough.

Middle years

Physically active more than passively reflective, Dragons nevertheless are resourceful creatures who can turn their hand to almost anything. Prince Edward first showed promise as the only true intellectual member of the Queen's children. But it soon emerged that Edward's style was one of an action man. He won a gold medal in his father's award scheme—a considerable achievement since Philip is not an easy man to please—and later entered the marines, after passing any number of gruelling physical tests. The fact that he quit his career in the marines in early 1987 says even more about Edward's animal sign. Dragons have an almost pathological fear of being locked up and find any routine a curb to their demands for a chain-free psyche. Army life is nothing if not routine and whereas some may find square bashing and the all-male environment to their liking, the Dragon sign is not one. Edward was criticized for quitting and portrayed in the press as a namby-pamby. But the tough part is getting into the marines, not getting out; he was selected with 30 others, from 2,000 hopefuls. Rightly, Edward saw years of meaningless slog as a needless test of his rôle, which he must have now discovered is simply to be himself. Dragons don't actually need to prove themselves unless others demand it. This does not mean that a Dragon like Prince Edward will shirk responsibility, but he must feel what he is doing has some point before committing himself. Then the Dragon will give 101 per cent. This is a feature of the Dragon's influence which went a long way to convince Andrew Lloyd Webber to employ Edward in his Really Useful Theatre Company in January 1988. Lloyd Webber, by the way, is a Rat and the Chinese are emphatic about it: Rats love Dragons.

Another illustration of how committed a Dragon can easily become was seen when Edward organized the royal charity version of 'It's a Knockout'. It also served to underline just how hot-headed Dragons behave when they fail to get full recognition for their contributions. At the press conference after the royal knockout show had been recorded, Edward asked a typically hard-nosed bunch of Fleet Street reporters what they had thought of it. Their response was, not unexpectedly, lukewarm— a few murmurs and not much more. Edward's reaction was instant. He got up, and said icily, 'Well thanks very much!' He then stormed out to his helicopter, telling photographers on the way, 'One of these days you lot are going to learn some manners'.

Yet another example of the Dragon's fiery tongue happened at the time Edward was asked about the press treatment of brother Andrew's relationship with Koo Stark. 'Despicable,' he said, 'Not only did they hound him over the affair; they actually hounded him to such an extent that he had to stop the holiday. To treat someone like that—who's just come back from serving their country—is absolutely despicable!'

The Chinese say that a Dragon's middle years, once they have got their self-confidence running in top gear, will offer endless opportunities. But Dragons make poor subordinates; they do things their way or not at all. Edward obviously understands this as it was a side of his Dragon's influence which came to light when he was a student at Cambridge. 'I very much enjoyed running my life the way I wanted to,' he said, 'I have cooked for myself. I am incredibly modest—but I tell you I am an excellent cook.' Personally, I have yet to meet a Dragon who has the faintest idea of what modesty means. It is like hoping to meet a Tiger without stripes.

Highly sensual, Dragons tend to make both friends and enemies with astonishing ease. Both Rats and Dragons have a very highly developed sexual nature but whereas the Rat seduces by charm, Dragons rely on self-assurance—I love me, why don't you? Forming strong physical relationships is high on the Dragon's list of priorities and Edward has already shown signs that he happily intends to submit to his animal influence. One name who has been linked with Edward's is Eleanor Weightman, daughter of an ICI executive. The couple were inseparable for almost a year and it was thought by some that an engagement was on the cards. Eleanor is a year younger than Edward, which makes her a Snake. This is a perfect match as the Chinese say emphatically that Dragons adore Snakes and are easily bewitched by them. But unless pressed, Dragon males do not rush into marriage. Life with a mortgage, wife, job, and a couple of young children is a state which, if experienced too early, tends to end up another routine-bound cage. If the Chinese Horoscopes are correct about the Dragon personality, Edward will not marry in his twenties unless forced to do so by his family.

The future

Unless a Dragon is able to remain the centre of everyone's attention the Chinese foretell that old age will find the carnival leader a pitiful creature. Dragons quickly go to seed, but they are blessed with a strong sense of humour. This they use to draw attention to themselves and Prince Edward is no exception. In this Dragon's case, humour expresses itself in playing practical jokes, like the time Edward upstaged his brother Andrew's wedding rehearsal by turning up with his arm in a sling. Then there was the famous case of his pretending to be drunk at a wine tasting. Neither prank would rate next to a sketch from 'Monty Python' or 'Alas Smith and Jones', but some people found them amusing.

How Edward's days end depends very much on what he does now. The Chinese say that the Dragon, along with the Snake, are karmic signs and that they reap what they sow. Fortunately, the trump card in the Dragon's hand is that they are born under the sign of luck. No matter how many wrong turnings they make, there is always a way out. As Edward himself has pointed out, 'I am one of the lucky ones. I have obviously had a few pitfalls along the way and made mistakes, but then again if one does make mistakes there is still someone to pick you up.'

In ancient China, it would be impossible to ignore the son of an Emperor who was born in a Dragon year. My feeling is that as the Dragon finds his feet, Prince Edward will seldom be far from the centre of the royal picture.

6
Queen Elizabeth II and the Duke of Edinburgh

The Queen
Birthdate: 21 April 1926
Born in the Year of the Tiger

In terms of the Chinese Horoscopes, there is a sense in which all royals are like caged animals. Some, like the central members of the Royal Family, could be described as born in captivity, while those who marry in might be said to resemble captured animals. Behind bars, animals are incapable of secrecy and the public are free to view them whenever they desire. Yet at the same time, such an existence blunts an animal's deeper instincts. Deprived of their natural surroundings, caged animals offer us an inadequate, and sometimes quite false, impression of their true nature. However, no matter how pampered and cosseted, or how far they deviate from their normal patterns of behaviour, caged animals can never be entirely free of their natural instincts. Caged or otherwise this is also true of Chinese animal signs. And, as we shall discover, this is particularly true of Her Majesty Queen Elizabeth.

Once 'caged' the more outgoing side of an animal's influence may easily become inverted. Dogs bite, Cats scratch, and and the normally generous Tiger frequently becomes miserly and mean. Indeed, it is difficult to understand why the Queen, the world's richest woman with a personal fortune estimated at over £3 billion, asks that the pots containing the plants she gives to her Windsor staff at Christmas be returned as 'they cost money'. But the story doesn't end there. When the Queen visited Africa in 1956, she and Prince Philip adopted a number of leper children and have paid for their medical and other expenses ever since. Both extremes represent two sides of the same coin. For all the deviations in character they might display, a Tiger's full influence will shine through. Her Majesty the Queen, is a Tiger who has amply illustrated both the positive and negative traits of her animal sign during her long and most public of all reigns.

Early years

The year the Queen was born, 1926, was vintage Tiger. Not only was it the birth year of some great Tiger personalities—Marilyn Monroe, Tony Bennett, and Dylan Thomas to name but a few—there were some typical Tigerish events. Gertrude Ederle was the first woman to swim the English Channel (in 14½ hours), Richard Byrd was the first man to fly over the North Pole, and, in Australia, the Victoria cricket team scored a record 1107 runs against New South Wales.

Normally speaking, Tiger people are rebellious and vigorous. They like leading a small band or group of people and being in at the sharp end. To be placed as supreme head or overlord is not what Tigers want. Nor is it a position in which they usually flourish. To be the King, or in the case of Elizabeth Windsor, the Queen, runs against the grain and deprives the Tiger of his or her natural urges. But fortunately for the young Princess Elizabeth, her earliest years were spent in an atmosphere which was relatively more sympathetic to the Tiger sign. As a child she grew up without even a distant thought that she would one day be Queen. Until her uncle, King Edward VIII, abdicated in 1936 (the Year of the opportunist Rat) the Queen believed her life would be conducted a long way from the throne and its relentless public attention.

However unpredictable, Tiger children tend to be strong-willed and extremely active. At the outbreak of the last war, the Queen insisted she play a role. In 1942, in spite of her father's strict wishes to the contrary, the 16-year-old Elizabeth insisted that she become a volunteer nurse. King George VI refused, and on that occasion got his way. But in the spring of 1945, Elizabeth finally broke free and joined the Auxiliary Territorial Service as a Second Subaltern. At 18, the Tiger Princess was determined to get her stripes!

Headstrong and self-aware, young Tigers are nevertheless popular. They are bright and very quick to learn. The young Tiger Princess was no exception.

Under the guiding hand of her famous governess, Miss Crawford (born in the Year of the Rooster, as is Prince Philip), each week Elizabeth would be shown a painting from the collection of royal masterpieces—a Rubens one week, a Canalletto the next. It is said that her family were astonished by how quickly young Elizabeth learned the names of the artists and was able to distinguish one work from another. As with all Tigers, Elizabeth expressed the need for self-awareness early. While attending a concert with her grandmother, Queen Mary, the Tiger Princess was asked if she would prefer to go home. 'Oh, no, granny,' Elizabeth replied, 'We can't leave before the end. Think of all the people who will be waiting to see us outside.'

Tigers tend to be popular from the very beginning, and this was certainly true of the young Elizabeth. Returning from the coronation of her father, George VI, the coach carrying Elizabeth, her sister Margaret, and the old Queen Mary registered the loudest cheers. Elizabeth was just 11 years old. Yet in spite of their instant appeal, Tigers of all ages tend to run out of steam. A fast start is usually following by a painfully slow end. Some Tigers show promise early and then fade, while others have regular highs and lows; a life of ups and down. From this point of view it might be argued that the Queen was never more happy than when she viewed her future from that coronation coach. However, as events turned out she was soon to become all too aware of the problems that face a Tiger placed on the throne. For most animal signs, the transition from the early to middle years is a slow one. For Elizabeth, we know the exact hour, day, week, and year her life changed forever. It happened on Friday 11 December 1936 when, following her uncle's abdication, Princess Elizabeth officially became heir to the throne.

Middle years

Although a number of memorable events have dominated the Tiger Queen's middle years, not all of them have been auspicious. Her four children, with the exception of the Dragon Edward, were not born under compatible signs. The Queen's marriage to Philip in 1947, in the Year of the Pig, was auspicious but the crowning moment, quite literally, of Her Majesty's life was not. The Queen's coronation took place on 2 June 1953. This was the Year of the Snake, and Tigers only merit a maximum of two out of five stars for success in a Snake year.

In China, the year people are born, marry, have children, and, in rare instances, get crowned emperor are all considered in relationship to the 12 animal signs. To marry in a Tiger year, for example is thought highly inauspicious and Chinese of all signs would rather wait than get married in such an inauspicious year. With this in mind, it might be said that the Queen's role as monarch has not been easy. There is a sense in which the frequently possessive Snake has entwined itself around the outgoing and vigorous Tiger. But whatever the Snake's hold, the Tiger Queen has done a great deal to allow her influencing sign as much freedom as possible. Tigers are born under the sign of courage and it is a pronounced feature. An example of the Queen's courage, and there are many, was seen during her visit to Canada in 1964. Assassination threats by extremists were taken seriously by her hosts, but the Queen was undeterred. She refused then, and continues to refuse, motorcycles either flanking her car or in front. Her Majesty considers them a hindrance to her coming in contact with those who line the route, some of whom have waited hours, and even days, to glimpse her as she drives by.

For a Tiger, even a caged one, the strongest instinct is to lead from the front. To be a boss who is an active part of the team is ideal. Tigers know their own mind and are not easily dissuaded, as Harold Macmillan, a sympathetic horse, observed about the Queen. He wrote in his diary: 'The Queen has been absolutely determined all through. She is impatient of the attitude towards her to treat her as a *woman*, a film star or a mascot. She loves her duty and means to be a Queen, not a puppet.'

Even so, the Queen *is* a woman, and as such has one very common female Tiger trait. The Chinese say that Tiger women dress smartly, with just a hint of 'look at me'. But they never dress to hide their identity. The way they reveal that the Tiger likes to be noticed is not through fabrics or designer outfits. Instead, Tiger ladies will often set off a suit with a splash of unexpected colour—a headscarf or expensive shoes. In the case of the Queen, it is her jewel box which gives the game away. When I met the Queen, at the bi-centenary celebration of *The Times*, I noticed her diamond and pearl brooch glittering under the photographers' flash lights. I later learned that it had been a gift to her grandmother and was worth roughly a quarter of a million pounds. Her Majesty's suit, I was also informed, was poor by comparison—a dull 10-year-old Norman Hartnell number that had seen a great many public functions.

With so many clearly defined characteristics, it is nevertheless the Tiger's sense of duty that has expressed itself most often in Her Majesty's public affairs. And her devotion to duty has never been more in evidence than in the Queen's attitude to the British monarchy. As she once said, with typical Tiger keenness, 'The strongest bonds of all are those which are recorded not on documents but in the hearts of the people who share the same beliefs and the same aims'. Those close to Her Majesty are unanimous; the Queen has been a central figure in re-establishing the British monarchy's reputation in the eyes of the world. Following the abdication of Edward VIII, the monarchy was in tatters. The former King's behaviour had struck a terrible blow to the seemingly unshakeable English crown. Britain's critics saw it as a chance to sneer and the world as a whole lost confidence in Britain's position as a moral leader. The moment it became clear that Elizabeth would one day be Queen she decided there and then that the English throne would never again be held in such low esteem. With the single-mindedness, energy, and courage that characterizes the Tiger, the Queen has, through her middle years, rebuilt the Royal Family's image to a point where they now dominate the world stage. On her accession, the fact that the raw, yet clearly determined Queen accepted *all* her father's often demanding appointments is a notable example of the headstrong Tiger's influence. However, the role of her Rooster husband, Prince Philip in this massive exercise in royal public relations is not to be underestimated. As we shall see later, in the section on their compatibility, his contribution to the remodelled monarchy has been inestimable.

The future

The general feeling about Her Majesty handing the throne to Charles is that it won't be for some time. The Chinese Horoscopes would endorse that view and add that only a Dragon year would be entirely auspicious for such an event. This would see the coronation of Prince Charles in either the year 2000 or 2012. But Tiger people do not retire unless it is absolutely essential and I do not see the Queen as an exception to this rule. Tigers throughout history have hung on, long after common sense has told them they no longer have the strength to do so. Joe Louis, the great heavyweight champion, was forever retiring only to make yet another fruitless comeback. Tigers also love to be at the sharp end. Lord Nelson was another typical Tiger who just had to be on the deck of his flagship at the battle of Trafalgar. Had he stayed in the background, where there was little or no danger he would have certainly survived. As it was, his need to be where the action was cost him his life.

Given that the Queen, now in her sixties, remains on the throne for the foreseeable future, it might be reasonably concluded that she has entered the third of the Tiger's three phases. As the beginning of the Queen's middle years was marked by George VI's coronation and the implication that she would herself one day be Queen, so the final period of Her Majesty's reign can also be pin-pointed by an auspicious event. The Queen's trip to China in 1986, the year of the Tiger, was both an historic occasion of huge significance and a glittering success. Although the visit had been planned for years, I have no doubt that the Chinese knew the Queen's birth sign and made the invitation accordingly—it would be *most* auspicious for a Tiger Queen to visit China in a Tiger year. Many royal visits are quickly forgotten. As important as some state visits may have been at the time, others, grander perhaps, frequently overtake them. But Her Majesty's trip to China, for the Chinese if no one else, will remain an ever-present memory.

Although her foreign and domestic visits are made as comfortable as humanly possible, there can be no doubt that trips like the one to China are extremely exhausting—even for a Tiger. I expect the Queen to cut down on public appearances and spend longer with her beloved dogs and horses. Interestingly, two of the Queen's best seasons as a race-horse owner were during highly auspicious years. In the Dog year of 1958, Pall Mall won the 2,000 Guineas and in 1974, a Tiger year, Highclere romped home to take the 1,000 Guineas.

However well Tigers and Horses may fare in business partnerships, in terms of all round compatibility, Tigers and Dogs have the highest rating. A Dog, in fact, is the only sign whose relationship with a Tiger gets five stars for lasting the distance. Many observers say that the Prime Minister who the Queen felt most at home with was Winston Churchill, who himself was born in a Dog year. It is an established fact that the Queen is never more contented than when surrounded by her faithful Corgis. If the Chinese Horoscopes are correct, as the Queen's children grow ever-more distant and her family circle breaks up, she will look more and more to her devoted dogs for solace and companionship. All parents face this sometimes painful period and it is a fact of life that we now see Her Majesty heading gracefully towards her final phase. But her loyal subjects can derive much comfort from oriental wisdom and its observations about Tiger people. The Chinese Horoscopes say that if Tigers overcome the dangers that face them in middle life, old age offers all that their hearts desire. In the case of the Queen, this will certainly mean many more happy and glorious years.

The Duke of Edinburgh
Birthdate: 10 June 1921
Born in the Year of the Rooster

All 12 animal signs have an introvert and extravert side, although in the case of the Dragon, Tiger, Pig, and Horse, an introvert personality is rare. With a tiny handful of exceptions, male Roosters are almost always extravert. In the main they are the chap in the bar that slaps you on the back, the mess hall braggart, the show-off at the Christmas party. Roosters jump up on the five-bar gate and herald dusk and dawn, and people born under their influence can't stop themselves from cock-a-doodle-dooing. Roosters are born under the sign of candour and the Chinese say the Rooster is a military sign. In addition to their sometimes unwelcome frankness Roosters cannot resist getting into a uniform whenever the chance presents itself. Put together the Rooster's candour and wardrobe packed tight with tunics, plumed hats, and medals, and you have an extremely short but perfect description of the Duke of Edinburgh.

If the Queen is a caged Tiger, then Prince Philip is perhaps a free-range Rooster; certainly his swagger and candid talking does not square with the image of the pathetic battery hen. We have only to recall the royal visit of the Queen and Duke of Edinburgh to China in 1986 to see the Duke's Rooster influence in action. Although the trip was a magnificent success, there were one or two minor hiccups. Not unexpectedly, it was the candid and outspoken Rooster Prince who was responsible. References to 'slitty eyes' and calling Peking 'ugly' were his alleged remarks and, as the Chinese would point out, made as a direct result of his influencing Rooster sign. But the Duke's observations were not taken seriously in China. As befits their national symbol, China's leader, Mr Deng Xiaoping was born in the year of the Dragon. Since Dragons have a five-star relationship with all Roosters the incident was officially laughed off.

Early years

The year Prince Philip was born, 1921, was typical, with a strong Rooster emphasis on military matters. There were serious riots in Egypt, and Greece, totally against the wishes of the League of Nations, declared war on Turkey. A peace treaty with Britain resulted in the Irish Free State. But Roosters have a keen social awareness at times. There were signs of this influence in 1921. It was the year that two Canadians isolated insulin at the University of Toronto, while in Britain, the British held its first Poppy Day.

The Chinese say that the early years of a Rooster's life will usually prove the most contented. In spite of a sticky start, this does indeed seem to have been true in Prince Philip's case. Although he was uprooted from his native Greece while still a baby, the son of Prince Andrew of Greece and Princess Alice of Battenberg quickly found a sympathetic host in Britain—his mother, after all, was the sister of Lord Mountbatten. Uncle Louis was born in a Rat year, and Rats are nature's charmers. Rats are opportunists to a very marked degree but the Chinese say their advice is always worth taking. Over the years, Philip has learned a great deal about the way Rats operate; two of his sons, his mother-in-law and his son-in-law, to name but a few of his relations, were all born in a Rat year. But no Rat has played a more important and influential role in Philip's life than his Uncle Louis. And it must be emphasized, in spite of the low marks opportunist Rat and candid Rooster achieve for compatibility at practically every level. As a result of Louis Mountbatten's careful guidance and the opportunism of his governing sign, Prince Philip of Greece was not only provided with a proper English name—his uncle's—but with an open door to the British Royal Family. It was Uncle Dickie—as Louis Mountbatten was affectionately known by his family—who, acting as matchmaker, was responsible for Philip meeting Elizabeth.

Prior to Philip's first glimpse of his future bride (she was thirteen, he eighteen), the Rooster's influence had already made its presence firmly felt. At Gordonstoun, where the young Prince was one of the first intake of pupils, the Rooster's cock-sure confidence, tinged by the fact that Roosters sometimes promise more than they can deliver, was much in evidence. Headmaster, Kurt Hahn wrote; 'Prince Philip's leadership qualities are most noticeable, though marred at times by impatience and intolerance'.

As with many Rooster men, the military world full of rituals and swagger—not to mention getting in and out of uniform—proved irresistible to the young Philip. Again with Mountbatten as his mentor, Philip enrolled at the Royal Naval College, Dartmouth, where he was an outstanding cadet. The Prince's period as a naval officer provides a clear insight as to how deeply the Rooster's influence can penetrate. For example, an illustration of the Rooster's incorruptibility can be found at the time when Philip, then plain Lieutenant Mountbatten, had failed an important naval examination paper. It transpired, via the Prince's equerry that Admiral Sir Arthur John Power was keen to rectify matters and re-mark the paper. Philip exploded when he heard. 'If they try to fix it,' he told his equerry, Michael Parker, 'I quit the Navy for good!' The Rooster Prince sat the examination a second time and passed easily.

Middle and future years

The three stages of life are sometimes difficult to distinguish. Clear as they may be in retrospect, at the time they might easily be seen as merging seamlessly one into the other. But for a royal, life is mapped out by certain immutable events. A coronation is one such occasion. Royal births, deaths, and weddings are others. Such events can dramatically alter the life of a member of the Royal Family. The abdication of Edward VIII and the death of King George VI completely changed the role of Princess Elizabeth. Although both events directly affected the Duke of Edinburgh's life, his middle and future phases have been linked to one single event—his marriage to the Queen. When they married in 1947, the Year of the Pig (auspicious for both Rooster Prince and Tiger Princess) the Duke relinquished certain rights. The rigid routine of being the Queen's consort would replace forever his former freedoms. But the Chinese Horoscopes suggest that such restrictions are perfect for the Rooster temperament. A well-ordered and organized lifestyle is what Roosters crave. What's more they thrive when the initiative is held by another positive-thinking sign. In this case, since the sign in question is a Tiger—an unlikely confederate in some circumstances, but strong in others—it simplifies matters to evaluate Prince Philip's second and third phases not as himself but as the Queen's marriage partner. Indeed, apart from his polo and sailing interests, his life has been entirely involved with that of the Queen. And their life together, even in spite of the fact they have their own interests, has been extremely close.

The Queen and the Duke of Edinburgh as marriage partners

The animals that influence the Queen and Duke of Edinburgh could not be more different. Whereas Tigers are beasts of the jungle, the Rooster is a farmyard creature. However, in the scale of compatibility Tigers and Roosters score three out of five stars. This is a comparatively high mark since both signs, particularly the Tiger, find relationships difficult and have few signs to turn to for a lasting relationship. In the case of the Queen and Prince

Philip, their compatibility is helped by the fact that both their signs have one significant characteristic in common: bravery. Tigers and Roosters are, some would say, recklessly brave. Although bravery is not an obviously important ingredient to a contemporary monarch—no sword waving on the battlefield these days—there are many occasions when courage of a less obvious kind is required.

When the Tiger Queen took the brave decision to devote her life to rebuilding the image of the British monarchy, she required a very special type of person to share her revolutionary ambition. The Rooster is such a creature. Needing a strong goal to inspire them, Roosters are not ones to give up easily when there is a fight, as anyone who has had the horrifying experience of watching a cock-fight will verify. And if they boast in public, Roosters are deeply private about their personal life. His sense of privacy has been a great help to Her Majesty, who has benefited hugely from Philip's direction and guidance, especially in matters of her unique public-cum-private profile. It was Philip, for example, who inspired the memorable image-boosting film, *Royal Family*, shown on BBC TV during the late sixties. Even so, the Rooster's candour was never very far from the proceedings. 'Don't bring your bloody cameras so close to the Queen', the Duke yelled at Richard Cawston, the film's director and producer. This remark joined a long list of candid classics, beginning with his outspoken observation: 'The *Daily Express* is a bloody awful newspaper'.

Money is another subject on which the Rooster has a strong opinion. Most spend it at once, others save every penny. Philip is patently a prudent Rooster. The monarchy would be in the red by 1970, the Prince said bluntly in 1969. The Rooster was asking for more and got it. Those in the know say it was largely due to this revealing statement, made in the light of rampant inflation that the Civil List was extensively reviewed.

Because both signs are very different and at the same time strong individuals, a successful marriage between Roosters and Tigers requires the tacit understanding that such individuality must at all times be given respect. The need to be free to pursue personal activities is paramount to such a relationship, yet no two people could be more different: he loves public speaking, she hates it; she loves the races, he prefers sailing; she adores walking the dogs, he would rather be out on the grouse moor with a shotgun. As the Chinese Horoscopes explain, 'Tiger and Rooster have little in common, but what they have is solid gold'.

During an eventful, and not always easy, period of history, the Queen and Prince Philip have been blessed with much good fortune, especially where their personal lives are concerned. Their marriage has proved strong enough for both Rooster and Tiger to live in their private worlds without too much hindrance or criticism. From the very beginning they chose to donate time and space for each other to breathe in. For example, their decision to sleep in separate but adjoining bedrooms was mutual. That they remain such good friends is not only a tribute to their continuing respect for each other's qualities but an acceptance of their two markedly different animal influences.

The Queen and the Duke of Edinburgh as parents

The Chinese argue that the educational styles of Rooster and Tiger parent are at opposite ends of the pole. Tigers make first-rate parents. They teach by example and are fountains of information and encouragement. Tiger mums and dads are story-tellers, original folk who place an emphasis on individuality. Roosters, on the other hand, are moralists. They care more about discipline than truth and insist that their children conform. This is especially true of Rooster fathers.

In the case of the Queen and Prince Philip, the general view is that the responsibility for their children's education has been shared, seemingly without any compromise. In common with Roosters everywhere, Philip wanted a traditional education for his four children. As a result all the boys were sent to Philip's old school. Since Gordonstoun happened to be open-minded and progressive, two qualities with which the Tiger can easily identify, the Queen was in total agreement. It is also typical of the rebellious Tiger to break with tradition, as did the Queen when she became the first ever monarch to send the heir to the throne to school. In any other age, Prince Charles would have been educated at home but Charles, like his sister and two brothers, was sent away. Charles at least, seems to have recognized the good sense of his parents' choice of school. 'I believe it taught me a great deal about myself and my own abilities,' he said, 'and it taught me to take challenges and initiatives.'

In spite of the understanding between Tiger mother and Rooster father, the Chinese Horoscopes say the matter doesn't end there. For a truly happy family the signs of children *and* parents have to be taken into account. But here, unfortunately, the news is not terribly auspicious. Charles and Andrew are both Rat signs, Anne is a Tiger, and Edward a Dragon. Rats get zero stars with a Tiger parent and only two stars with a Rooster, which is not at all satisfactory and means a lot of misunderstanding. Tiger and Tiger gets minus points as does Tiger and Rooster; poor Anne. However, things look up for the Dragon Edward—he gets five out of five with Tiger mother and Rooster father! Well, the Dragon *is* born under the sign of luck.

7
Princess Margaret and Lord Snowdon

Princess Margaret
Birthdate: 21 August 1930
Born in the Year of the Horse

Lord Snowdon
Birthdate: 7 March 1930
Born in the Year of the Horse

In addition to their pronounced spirit of independence, Horses are extremely practical people brimming over with stamina. These qualities—independence, practicality, and stamina were much in evidence in 1930, the year that Margaret and Tony were born. It was the year that one of the most practical innovations of all time, Birdseye frozen food, went on sale. In Arizona, after centuries of scanning the heavens, the planet Pluto was discovered by the Lowell Observatory, and in May, Amy Johnson became the first woman to fly solo from London to Darwin, Australia. Horses are born under the twin signs of elegance and ardour. Throughout their life together and following their divorce, both Margaret and Tony have displayed these two sharply defined characteristics to a very marked degree.

126

Early years

The Chinese Horoscopes point out that the Horse's independent nature will express itself from an early age and that parental restrictions, should there be any, will only serve to accelerate the young Horse's departure from the fold. Obviously, it would have been impossible for Margaret to leave her family, even if she had wanted to, but the Horse's strong personality and self-assurance made its presence felt right from the start. Horse women in particular have wonderfully witty minds and bags of style. Princess Margaret was no exception. Queen Mary, her grandmother and a tough lady to please socially, found her 'so outrageously amusing that one can't help encouraging her'.

Margaret was luckier than her sister Elizabeth in having one parent, her father, with whom she was totally compatible. Her father was a Goat, a sign which scores maximum points for compatibility with the Horse in every area of human relationships, and there is no question that Goat father and Horse daughter shared a very great deal. As John Wheeler Bennett, who wrote a biography of George VI, observed, 'She it was who could always make her father laugh, even when he was angry with her'.

Lord Snowdon's early years were typical of a young upper-class Brit. He was a product of private education; a system from which he emerged without much distinction. One school report read: 'Maybe he is interested in some subject, but it isn't a subject we teach here'. With the exception of coxing the light blues to victory in the 1950 Boat Race (Horses can be very physical), Lord Snowdon found nothing to tax the Horse's heightened sense of practicality at his prep school, at Eton, or later at Cambridge. It was only when he discovered a skill for taking photographs that his animal sign began to make its presence felt. Photography is nothing if not a practical art form. There's lighting, shutter speeds, film speeds, plus a million and one other details. To be a success means working longer hours than most people imagine, but the pay-off is that every photographer is his or her own boss—the work-loving Horse's most important requirement.

127

Although Horses are well known for suddenly becoming bored, even with something they have loved forever, Lord Snowdon has found photography a constant passion. It is both a form of liberation and solace for the Horse sign's ardent personality. But it is in the field of human relationships that Horses find themselves most frequently bored. The big love affair of today quickly becomes yesterday's yawn. This is certainly true in the case of Princess Margaret and Lord Snowdon, who have been noticeably bored, in turn, with each other and their numerous lovers.

Middle years

To a certain degree, Tony and Margaret were untypical Horses in that they were forced to wait until their early to mid twenties before announcing their independence. When it finally came for Tony, independence found expression through his stylish dress sense as much as in his modish and talked-about photography. He dressed in dark polo-necks worn with handsomely made jackets. As for Snowdon's pictures, at that time they were often of unusually beautiful moody models, taken in off-beat poses. For Margaret, independence took the unusual (for a royal) and rebellious form of smoking openly—sometimes 50 cigarettes a day—and drinking whenever and whatever she wanted. As jazz giant Louis Armstrong shrewdly, if somewhat colloquially, observed, 'Your princess is one hip chick'.

But there was a greater indication of Margaret's Horse influence, and one which more or less dominated her during the early middle years. Her 11-year wait to marry Peter Townsend was a massive demonstration of self-assurance and strongly underlined the Princess's independent nature. The Chinese say that a Horse's middle period will be mixed, with both love and finance posing problems. In Princess Margaret's case, her long and ultimately tragic affair with Group Captain Peter Townsend proves the point. Although it *did* end unhappily, there can be little doubt that Margaret tried every way she knew how to marry Townsend. The Horse in love is a powerful and sometimes frightening beast. With their normally dependable sense of logic thrown to the wind, Horses become weak and unsure of themselves. But the Horse's great stamina is ever present. This leaves the Horse in love acting a bit like the leader of a team pulling a run-away stage coach. As one close friend put it: 'The Princess in love is terribly demanding . . . dazzling as well as devouring'. Sadly for Margaret, should she have married Townsend, a Rat born in 1914, they would have made an even bigger hash of it—if that were possible. Rats and Horses score zero points for compatibility in practically every department.

Princess Margaret and Lord Snowdon as marriage partners

The Chinese Horoscopes are oddly ambivalent about two Horses getting married. On one hand, they say that their style and natural elegance, their wit and good sense will overcome most problems. On the other, they point a pair of Horses in opposite directions. Horses in love are different from Horses in a marriage and because the Horse is such an independent creature, only those who have outlined their personal boundaries carefully in advance should take the plunge. In other words, a Horse couple must take into account, and make provisions for, their overwhelming need to be independent before having the banns read. Any form of stable, fence, or harness will only serve as a wedge between them. Matters are not helped by the fact that one of the twin signs that Horses are born under is ardour. This means that Horses fall in love far too easily and too often for their own good. To add to the problem of a vulnerable heart, Horses are too easily loved in return.

It doesn't need a Chinese Horoscope to point out that Princess Margaret's and Lord Snowdon's marriage was a huge flop. With no boundaries of personal freedom drawn up to help protect them, these two Horses were clearly not destined to last the course together. But the lack of compatibility was quite spectacular, with Tony outstanding in the manner he adamantly refused to tow the royal line. From the very beginning, it was obvious that walking behind his wife at the opening of a factory in Slough or a shipyard in Jarrow was not his thing. It wasn't Margaret's thing either but it was her job. There were those who warned against a royal marrying a commoner, even a wealthy one (his grandfather was a millionaire stockbroker). But the real problem stemmed from the Horse's constant need to be free and, in most instances, to fall in love without restrictions. In this and all other areas, Tony's and Margaret's Horse-bound relationship followed the path laid down by the Chinese Horoscopes to the letter. In the early stages two Horses are expected to be fascinated by each other; their mutual vanity, a pronounced Horse trait, creating the strongest of physical bonds. As a friend of the time says now, 'What Snowdon had foremost in common with Princess Margaret could be put into three words—sex, sex, sex'.

Both during their marriage and since the divorce, Margaret and Tony were unable to prevent themselves forming a string of passionate relationships with partners drawn from a wide range of social groups. In Margaret's case, her men friends came mainly from the world of show-biz and the arts, thus emphasizing something of the Horse's love of witty society, and the need to be seen as a front runner—a position granted naturally by her royal status. The names of Patrick Litchfield (Cat), Peter Sellers (Buffalo), Sir Frederick Ashton (Dragon), Jocelyn Stevens (Monkey) are just a handful of a long list who have been linked with Margaret, providing a variety of different friendships. All but the Monkey would have provided a more compatible partner than Tony. Yet, overall, Margaret is a poor judge and her affair with Roddy Llewellyn was a case in point. Roddy was born in the year of the Pig and is another no-hoper in the Horse relationship stakes. Fun at first, Pigs and Horses are no long-term match as Pigs tend to lean heavily on their partner. And to add to the difficulty, both animal signs are utterly helpless when gripped by love.

Lord Snowdon, following an involved relationship with Jacqueline Rufas Isaacs, a Dog who rates five stars with a Horse, married Lucy Lindsay-Hogg, the former wife of film producer and director, Michael Lindsay-Hogg. Lucy was born in 1941, the year of the Snake. Horses and Snakes score three stars out of five for compatibility, so Tony has at last got it right. Well, almost!

Princess Margaret and Lord Snowdon as parents

When Horses become parents they usually approach their role in the same practical manner they do everything else. Horses have warm hearts and love deeply, but in parenthood they tend to be a little reserved. It is as if there's a slender barrier that prevents a Horse gushing over their children, which can be both good and bad. Most Horse parents prefer to approach the task of education in common-sense terms, and there is seldom any place for sloppy sentiment. But the Chinese warn that male Horses will tend to put their job before their home, and in an age of liberated career-orientated women, the same is also true of lady Horses.

By all accounts, Margaret and Tony have not been over-generous in the time they have spent with their children. Of the two, Tony seems to have had the greatest influence, passing on his artistic gifts to both Viscount Linley and Lady Sarah. It was, one suspects, his decision to send his son to the John Makepeace School for Craftsmen in Wood, and not to Eton. In terms of the scale of compatibility, Horse parents have no understanding of a Buffalo child—Viscount Linley—but a four-star relationship with a Dragon. This seems to be true both in the case of Lady Sarah and the young Viscount.

Viscount Linley
Birthdate: 3 November 1961
Born in the Year of the Buffalo

Lady Sarah Armstrong-Jones
Birthdate: 1 May 1964
Born in the Year of the Dragon

Buffalo children are not easy to understand, and become less so if
you are a Horse parent. The powerful influence of the Buffalo
made its presence felt in Viscount Linley from an early age, and it
was clear that he would grow into a strong-willed individual who
knew his own mind. He has shown great skill as a carpenter, with
a distinct style. Unhappy to be tagged 'royal' he prefers to be
called simply 'David Linley', expecting to be judged by his work
rather than by his family's connections. Recently he has added the
skill of photography to his range. In 1987, he become the first
member of the Royal Family in direct line to the throne to have a
criminal record. A Brentford magistrate found him guilty of a
motoring offence and banned the 10th in line to the throne from
driving for six months. Buffaloes, it must be said, are complex
animals and they are driven by an inner compulsion that is
seldom, if ever, fully under control.

Lady Sarah has no such internal complexities. As a Dragon she
is filled with self-confidence, a quality which was evident as she
cycled alone through the busy London streets from her Kensington Palace home to Camberwell School of Arts and Crafts, where
she studied for a degree in fine art. Since it is a heavily masculine
sign, Dragon ladies have a tougher time than Dragon men but the
Chinese predict that no female Dragon will ever end up a wilting
violet. Dragons of both sexes make the most of every inch of talent
they possess. She is also a close friend of the Prince of Wales,
which is entirely to be expected. Dragons, say the Chinese

Horoscopes, are adored by the Rat. Charles is a Rat, which perhaps explains why Lady Sarah was chosen to be a bridesmaid at his wedding.

According to the Chinese Horoscope, Margaret's and Tony's two children, Buffalo and Dragon, are destined to make their names in the world, and that they will do so quite independently of the tight royal circle that spawned them. However, when Charles becomes King, I fully expect Lady Sarah to be given a central role in the new reign, one I am certain she will relish.

8
King George VI and Queen Elizabeth the Queen Mother

HM King George VI
Birthdate: 14 December 1895
Born in the Year of the Goat

HM Queen Elizabeth the Queen Mother
Birthdate: 4 August 1900
Born in the Year of the Rat

Of the 12 signs that make up the Chinese Horoscope, the Goat stands out as one of the most feminine. They have shy and gentle manners, on the whole, and the people of the East look to the Goat as a harbinger of peace. Once tethered, the Goat exudes confidence. Born under the sign of art, the Goat's influence expresses itself most profoundly in the field of the performing arts. No other animal enjoys the comforts and beauty life can offer, or does so much to obtain them. Goats, say the Chinese Horoscopes, adore the world of the senses—good food, fine clothes, and beautiful surroundings. It is therefore particularly ironic that George VI, a shy and gentle Goat, should have ascended to the throne at a time when beauty, comfort, and, more important by far, peace, were nowhere to be found.

Although life improved with age for Bertie, as the King was affectionately called, he experienced a large degree of frustration and pain, especially during the early years. For example, Goat children tend to cling to their parents and require a great deal of moral and intellectual guidance if they hope to mature into self-reliant adults. In this respect Bertie could not have had a more inauspicious father. George V dominated the young Goat, casting a shadow over his son's self-confidence which was only lifted by Bertie's future wife.

George V was a Buffalo and a traditionalist of the most reactionary kind. Typically, Bertie's father's animal influence found a number of quirky means of expressing itself. The King used the same collar stud and hair brush for 50 years and was punctual to the point of an obsession. Above all, he loved shooting and stamp collecting and would spend hours engrossed in albums. Of George V's general behaviour, the writer Harold Nicolson once observed pithily, 'For seventeen years he did nothing at all but kill animals and stick in stamps'. As the Chinese Horoscopes emphasize, as a Buffalo King George V had a zero understanding of his Goat son. Buffaloes rely on solid tradition and large helpings of discipline to educate their offspring. Sadly, this was true of Bertie's Buffalo father as the famous case of his futile and brutal attempt to cure his son's knock knees illustrates. To combat this 'deformity', George V stuck the young boy's legs in splints and forced him to sit in an armchair for hours on end. The pain was so intense that it made the helpless child weep. And there is another instance of the Buffalo's often clumsy approach to rid life of its ills. Bertie was left handed so his father forced him under threat to write with his right hand. Not surprisingly, Bertie developed a terrible stammer which was to stay with him through his life. Tethering a young Goat with a stout length of rope is one thing, but strangling him with it is another.

Yet for all his father's ignorance and lack of understanding, Bertie wasn't completely without allies among the animal signs. His brother David (the future Edward VIII), a Horse, and his Cat mother Queen Mary, were both highly compatible. Cats share the Goat's love of beauty and although it might raise a few eyebrows one shouldn't be too shocked to discover that Queen Mary taught all her children, including the boys, needlepoint. Visitors to royal palaces would often find David and Bertie happily passing away their afternoons with needle and thread. Although Cat parents can sometimes be a little too reserved emotionally with their children—which was certainly true of Queen Mary—their teaching skills are nevertheless blessed with great refinement.

Of all Bertie's close family, David provided a perfect partner. As the Chinese point out, there are few more compatible partnerships than a Horse and a Goat. The Horse is able to tether the Goat without fuss or frills. In return, the Goat's gentle nature can calm the Horse's ardour. But in all relationships, it is the Horse who leads. A recent revelation about the two brothers tells how the Duke of Windsor would continue to phone the King and tell him how to run the country long after he had abdicated.

For a Goat, the home and strong family ties are crucial if they are to enjoy a well-balanced life and it was only when Bertie was accepted by Lady Elizabeth Bowes-Lyon at the third time of asking that his fragile world began to take a more solid shape. A Rat and a Goat achieve almost full marks for compatibility in marriage, a situation which is made near perfect once a home and family are established. It is no wonder then that the lost Goat found his way under the intelligent guidance of the warm and passionate Rat. With Elizabeth at his side, Bertie blossomed. He lost much of his stammer and basking in the joy of his daughters found a new brand of confidence: 'Us four,' he would say. Formally hesitant to a painful degree, he now seemed to relish his rôle, performing in public with something which at last resembled the Goat's natural character. On the famous American trip they made in the fifties, he and Elizabeth virtually invented the now indispensible walkabout—a term when given a moment's reflection, is tailor-made for the opportunist Rat and capricious Goat.

Indeed, the influence of the Queen Mother's Rat sign made its presence felt from the moment she entered public life. The wedding of Bertie and Elizabeth was the social event of the year and when the young bride arrived at Westminster she suddenly broke ranks and laid her bouquet on the tomb of the unknown warrior. It was the first of thousands of delightfully charming, warm-hearted, and spontaneous gestures that have made the Queen Mother so deeply loved. It was also a perfect example of all that is best in the Rat personality. And the wedding itself was an auspicious event. It took place in 1923, the year of the Pig. The Chinese would always encourage a wedding in a Pig year, especially if bride and groom are a Rat and a Goat, respectively. In addition to the fact there is much understanding between all three signs, it is believed that the Pig's influence creates both wealth and family unity. This again, would seem to fit the picture we have of King George VI, his wife, and family.

The Chinese say Rats adore sweet things and love to have their minds as well as their bodies stimulated. 'Sitting in bed eating chocolates and reading poems' is the way the Queen Mother once described her favourite pastime. Throughout her life, under the Rat's charming influence, the Queen Mother has won herself rank upon rank of devoted supporters. One of the first to fall under her spell was the Queen Mother's father-in-law, the Buffalo King, who once told Bertie, 'The better I know and the more I see of your dear little wife, the more charming I think she is and everyone falls in love with her'. As the Chinese explain, Buffaloes are often attracted by Rats. For once George V got it right.

9
The Duke and Duchess of Windsor

The Duke of Windsor
Birthdate: 23 June 1894
Born in the Year of the Horse

The Duchess of Windsor
Birthdate: 19 June 1896
Born in the Year of the Monkey

Remarkably, there have been two Monkey and Horse marriages in the house of Windsor during the last half century and, more remarkable still, neither Monkey women come from the British nobility. Princess Michael, the most recent Monkey to marry a royal, comes from a controversial Austrian background, while the late Duchess of Windsor, the Monkey who many saw as an intruder into British life at the time when she married King Edward VIII, was the daughter of a Baltimore businessman.

There is a sense in which Monkey ladies tend to trap their men, 99 per cent of the time being much too smart to get trapped themselves. This they do with a subtle mixture of sparkling wit, feigned concern and intellectual flattery, a cocktail of seduction which few males can resist. Observers at the time, for instance, told how it was Wallis's openly flirtatious behaviour that drove her first husband to drink. And since it is said that Monkeys of both sexes care very little about their reputations, their wit might easily be a touch near the bone. There are dozens of recorded instances of the Duchess of Windsor and her sexually spiced repartee. A classic concerns an ancient Celtic fertility statue in Devon. Wallis was explaining to a male guest that, 'it shows a gentleman in a state of violent erection. The townspeople were so embarrassed that they planted a hedge round it.' The guest asked 'Privet, I presume'. There was a short pause. 'No,' replied Wallis, 'I think it's honeysuckle.'

It is also said that Monkeys find long-term relationships a problem. Twice divorced, The Duchess of Windsor was born in full possession of all the Monkey's most seductive traits. Given her experience of men, and her wide range of Monkey skills, she found seducing her third husband easy. The love-sick Horse, Edward VIII, was a pushover.

Of all royal couples, none have lives which are better documented than those of the Duke and Duchess of Windsor. At every stage of their dramatic and highly public life together both Horse and Monkey created reams of information about their most personal feelings. Most revealing are the bundles of letters the couple sent to each other throughout the ordeal of the King's abdication. Here the Horse, always weak in love, is shown to be so in the extreme. On the other hand, the cool Monkey, full of self-control at all times, is never seen to be letting passion run away with her. A few lines taken at random give the full flavour of the Horse and Monkey in love. The Horse King seemed totally out of control when in December 1936, he wrote to Wallis:

> 'Everybody'—all of 'US' here—send all of 'YOU' oohs enormous oohs for Christmas and we are all of 'US' are so sad we can't send each other any presents. HE (I hide face) Eanum and Pig (I hide face again) and all the toys miss YOU ALL at LOO VIE more than I can say . . .

Wallis's replies were somewhat less gushing, as would be expected from the Monkey influence:

Something must be done to put it out of the people's mind in England that your family are against us. I can't stand up against this system of trying to make me an outcast in the world.

The Chinese Horoscopes explain that Horse men are natural leaders, confident and logical in many areas of life, except as we have seen, when in love. The Duke of Windsor was a perfect example of the Horse, both in and out of love. Horses are born under the twin signs of elegance and ardour, and it is commonly held that Horses of both sexes are usually endowed with a high sense of fashion. In his life, the Duke of Windsor introduced a new way to knot neckties (the Windsor) and gave the world the Prince of Wales check. No one would argue that Edward VIII was the best-dressed man of his day. He was certainly one of the most popular prior to his abdication. Few members of royalty can have had their names so flatteringly commemorated in a popular song; remember the hit 'I Danced with A Man Who Danced with a Girl Who Danced with the Prince of Wales'? When female Monkeys dress well, they do so mainly to create an effect. To impress is an inherent feature of the Monkey personality and during the years when people talked about the world's best-dressed woman, it is worth recalling that the Duchess of Windsor won the title 15 times in a row.

Horses and Monkeys are said to be vain creatures. They have a high opinion of their own considerable array of talents, and it could easily be that their mutual vanity acts as a bond, a lifeline thrown to each other at times when understanding runs short. In the case of Edward, the vain influence of his Horse sign split into two quite distinct types. There was a reflected vanity, which expressed itself by his giving the object of his love an endless flow of sometimes priceless gifts—jewels, cars, objets d'art, and so on, and the more conventional type which is purely self-regarding. An outstanding example of Edward's open vanity came to light when he was asked to adopt a right-facing pose for the new coins and stamps. The tradition is that each new monarch faces the opposite direction to the previous ruler. Edward would have none of it. The reason the King gave was that he parted his hair on the left and consequently preferred to have his left profile depicted. When told he had created a break in tradition, Edward replied, 'Why shouldn't I?'

In an earlier chapter, I said that kings and queens are a bit like caged animals, and that those who marry into the royal circle are like animals who have been captured. Following through with the analogy, the Duke and Duchess of Windsor more resemble creatures who, having been born in captivity, as a result of the King's abdication are suddenly set free. The consequence was that their natural instincts, many of which were never given a chance to develop, ran riot while some instincts showed themselves often in stunted form; others were simply inadequate to deal with life 'in the wild'. However, the Horse and Monkey are both extremely resourceful animals, and the Duke and Duchess of Windsor did the best they could. But they faced an uphill task, especially taking in the fact that Horse and Monkey are zero rated for compatibility in marriage. Yet, after reading the copious accounts of their life together, it is difficult not to see this Horse and Monkey as a pair of creatures who, cut off from their most crucial instincts for so long, ended up by treating each other as little more than twin mirrors to reflect their own vain self-indulgences. For an example of the Horse and Monkey surviving under the most negative influences, we need look no further.

10
Prince and Princess Michael of Kent

Prince Michael
Birthdate: 4 July 1942
Born in the Year of the Horse

Princess Michael
Birthdate: 15 January 1945
Born in the Year of the Monkey

Of all the signs, the Horse is unquestionably the most practical. Horses have clear minds and strong personalities which are underpinned by a cool sense of reason. They are not given to day-dreaming and are at their best when exercising their considerable physical abilities. But as we have seen in other Horses, royal and commoner, love is an area they have no control over. Once smitten, even by a casual romance, Horses become weak and unsure of themselves.

Although the year of Prince Michael's birth, 1942, was clouded by the war and the death of his father (born in the Year of the Tiger) in a flying accident, there was still evidence of the practical influence of the Horse. At Stagg Field at the University of Chicago, under physicists Enrico Fermi and Arthur Compton, the world's first ever nuclear chain reaction took place.

Prince Michael of Kent is a Horse from his bearded chin to his feet. Although somewhat overshadowed by his relatives from Buck House, not to mention his publicity prone wife, Prince Michael has nevertheless provided ample proof of his Horse's influence. During his 19-year term with the 11th Hussars, he distinguished himself as a Russian interpreter and enjoyed two spells with the Defence Intelligence staff. For most of his life, he has thrown himself into all kinds of physical activities. Two years after having taken up the sport, Prince Michael represented the Army and won the Army Two-Man Bobsleigh Championships. Even after suffering severe neck and chin injuries, he continued to race, driving the British four-man team. Even when he retired, Prince Michael stayed on as manager and now holds the position of president of the British Bobsleigh Association. Since then, the Horse influence has continued to express itself in a typically physical manner; Prince Michael making his mark as a rally driver, motor cyclist and pilot.

It is a remarkable fact that two key royal figures, both Horses, have in recent times married Monkey women who were not born royal. Wallis Simpson was a Monkey and so is Princess Michael. And the parallel with the Duchess of Windsor has been noted by the perceptive writer on royalty, Audrey Whiting. In her book, *The Kents* she makes the following observation.

> For him, (Prince Michael) the cosmopolitan Marie-Christine possessed some of the powerful characteristics which had attracted his Uncle David, when he was the Prince of Wales, to Mrs Simpson. She was witty, clever and highly organized in her personal life. With her self-confidence she was able to take anyone in her stride, royal or otherwise.

By the way, if Koo Stark had married Prince Andrew, she would have made a third. Although the Monkey and Rat, Koo and Andrew's signs, are highly compatible, the Horse and the Monkey have absolutely no understanding and are ranked at the bottom of the compatibility chart alongside Tiger and Buffalo.

Monkeys are born under the sign of fantasy. As a result they have a highly personal view of reality. It follows that a Monkey's concept of fact and fiction is less black and white than most other people's. Truth, to put it bluntly, is not the Monkey's strongest point. The Chinese believe Princess Michael's influencing animal to be the nearest to mankind and that all the worst and best of our behaviour is seen, often exaggerated in the Monkey influence. Monkeys make great mimics, they are expert wheeler-dealers, and it is held that Monkey women have the ability to trick people into believing what they say.

Unfortunately for Princess Michael, the press's handling of her 'private' life has not always been flattering. Their discovery that her father had been involved with the Nazi movement was a case in point. Furthermore, Princess Michael's subsequent denial that she had any knowledge of the fact did not ring true for many. And I have a personal account of how Princess Michael's ability to adapt quickly to changing circumstances once expressed itself. An Australian solicitor friend of my wife Gabrielle, knew Princess Michael as a teenager in Sydney. At that time, according to Gabrielle, the Princess spoke with a pronounced Australian drawl. You can imagine Gabrielle's surprise when she heard Princess Michael talking on British TV shortly after her marriage with an affected Central European accent. Then there was the embarrassing incident of her book, *Crowned in a Far Country*. After it was published and heralded by many as an original work, it emerged that Princess Michael had copied whole chunks from a number of other books and was forced to admit to plagiarism. To crown it all, in another far country there was the headline-hitting alleged affair with an American millionaire.

But the Monkey is nobody's fool, and if things get tough they are better equipped than most to get themselves out of a hole. They can turn the situation round to suit themselves in less time than it takes to leap from one branch to another. Amid all the accusations of plagiarist, adulteress and liar, Princess Michael disarmed her critics by a series of candid statements. The most pointed was: 'They need a soap opera to sell newspapers and they've got a hell of a soap opera with the Royal Family. They needed a bad girl and they've cast me in that rôle.' She also said, with typical Monkey vanity, 'I tend to land on my feet. You see, I have this tremendous instinct for self-preservation.' No wonder the Queen calls her 'Princess Pushy'.

The children

If the Horse and the Monkey score no marks for compatibility, matters improve considerably when their children are at home. Their son, Lord Frederick, was born on 6 April 1979, and Gabriella (Lady Ella) on 23 April 1981. Frederick is a Goat and Gabriella is a Rooster. A Horse father has a near perfect understanding of a Goat son and a better than average relationship with a Rooster daughter. Unfortunately for the Horse Prince, his Monkey wife does not enjoy the same high level of compatibility with their children. Although, Monkeys as a rule make extremely good parents, they have little or no understanding of either Goat or Rooster. And it's poor marks for understanding between the two children, which suggests a pretty gloomy home life for the Michaels of Kent. I am not surprised that the Monkey Princess is so fond of monkeying around.

11
The Duke and Duchess of Kent

The Duke of Kent
Birthdate: 19 October 1935
Born in the Year of the Pig

The Duchess of Kent
Birthdate: 22 February 1933
Born in the Year of the Rooster

Given the wide choice of marriage partners that greets the Pig—more than any other sign—Edward the Duke of Kent might have chosen a little more auspiciously. Although Pigs have a three-star relationship with a Rooster in love, the relationship drops a point after the wedding. As partners, Pigs and Roosters are both happiest in the farmyard, so to speak, and as long as the Pig works hard and respects the Rooster's need for privacy there is a one in three chance that the marriage will survive. So far, the Kents seem to have done a first-class job of illustrating the crucial point that the Chinese Horoscopes scale of compatibility is only a basic guide, and that when the boundaries of personal behaviour within the relationship have been agreed to on both sides, it can be dispensed with.

The problem facing Pigs is that when they fall in love they lose all self-control, and the Chinese say that they tend to wear their hearts on their sleeves. Edward was no exception. When he fell in love with Katherine he actually suggested that they elope. He added that they should 'hang the consequences', which is as typical a Piggy statement as you will find anywhere. But with equally typical Rooster conservatism, Katherine would not be rushed. Although some might spend as if there is no tomorrow, all Roosters hate to act rashly in matters of romance. Edward was to wait six years after their initial meeting before she finally agreed to become engaged. They married in 1961, the year of the Buffalo, and an auspicious one for both Roosters and Pigs.

With the Pig's fondness for dressing up—the Duke of Kent is a freemason Grand Master—Edward demonstrates his sign's most obvious characteristics in a number of departments. He works and plays hard, listing his hobbies, as skiing, riding, opera, photography, and private flying, which he shares with Fergie— another Royal Pig. When, as an Army officer, he was posted to Leeds, Edward was said to have yearned for London and its night spots. As a young Pig he couldn't resist socializing and all that went with it. In his early twenties he had a passion for fast cars and managed to crash at least two, once narrowly escaping death. In commerce, Pigs are believed to make money easily and it is in this field that the Duke of Kent has devoted most of his working life.

There has been much talk concerning the Duchess of Kent's health in recent years, mainly about her depression. But when viewed through her animal sign, Katherine would seem a quite different person from the one the press normally portrays. The media, as a whole, over-react terribly to any illness or set-back which might befall any member of the Royal Family. No matter how slight the sickness, press and TV manage to blow it up out of all proportion.

In the case of the Duchess of Kent, there is no question that she has suffered both grief and illness. The loss of her baby in 1977 was believed to have been the cause of the much discussed, but never fully substantiated, stories about Katherine's mental and physical health. But as one would expect from the Rooster personality, Katherine coped with her difficulties not by pretending that all was well, but by a candid appraisal of herself and circumstances. Unlike so many who are cushioned by wealth and/or privilege, those born in a Rooster year will always demand that they be left to stand on their own two feet. Brave and determined Roosters do not accept help from anyone, no matter how willing the hand. Luckily the Pig is one sign to whom the Rooster will respond, and many attribute Katherine's return to full health and an active life as a direct result of the patience and devotion shown to her by the Duke of Kent. Pigs cannot be faulted for their open-mindedness and generosity. In adversity both signs are asked to produce their best, and together, as in the case of the Kents, they very often achieve their goal.

Roosters are deeply conservative creatures with the highest possible moral overview. When in 1976, Katherine discovered she was pregnant once more, it was around the time of her 45th birthday. Not unnaturally there was talk of an abortion. But when the subject was put to her, Katherine replied with the outspoken moral candour which distinguishes the Rooster from all other signs. 'Human life is sacred,' she said, 'and uniquely valuable. It is a gift of God and, as such, must never be taken for granted.'

When any kind of danger threatens, a Rooster will fight it regardless. Although the Duchess was supported at all times through her series of low ebbs by a devoted family, it was ultimately due to Katherine's Rooster sign and its determined and indomitable spirit that she is once again playing a full rôle in the often arduous round of public duties. There was a perfect insight to the Rooster's powerful influence on the Duchess of Kent early in 1988. Millions of TV viewers watched as on the 'News at Ten' she entered the pathetic homes of uncared for pensioners and demanded we all share in solving the problems of the aged. 'Don't cry, don't cry, don't cry', she begged one sad old lady, fighting back the tears in her own eyes. By demanding strength in the face of adversity the Duchess illustrated the very best of the Rooster's generous, if sometimes unflexible, heart. It was a moving moment without the slightest hint of publicity-seeking sham.

The children

The Kents' children, George, Earl of St Andrews, a Tiger (born 26 June 1962), Lady Helen Windsor, a Dragon (born 28 April 1964), and Lord Nicholas Windsor, a Dog (born 25 July 1970) help to make the Kent family one of the most auspicious in the royal circle. Tigers get on extremely well with both Dragons and Dogs; in fact, they serve as a communicating link between them. Mother Roosters adore a Dragon child and Pig fathers have complete understanding of both Tiger and Dog offspring. And the Tiger is no back runner when it comes to a comprehension of father Pig. While still in short trousers, the young Earl was once asked what his father did for a living? With all the Tiger's presence of mind George replied, 'He changes in and out of uniform'. On 9 January 1987, George added to his list of rebellious acts when he became the first member of the Royal Family to marry in a register office. This he did because his bride, Sylvana is both a divorcee and a Catholic. But nothing stands in the way of true love for a Tiger. By marrying his Rooster wife George has relinquished any claim to the throne, and he was 17th in line. In terms of their animal signs, his marriage also mirrors the Queen's, a Rooster and Tiger. As with George's school reports, he could have done better.

Born in the same year as her Dragon cousins, Lady Sarah Armstrong-Jones and Prince Edward, Lady Helen Windsor will almost certainly step more into the public limelight during the four-year spell that began in 1987, the year of the Cat. The following years—Dragon, Snake, and Horse—are all splendid for Dragons and it will be difficult for her to keep out of the news. As we have seen Prince Edward develop an increasingly high profile, so Lady Helen Windsor will also make her mark. This she will do by a mixture of her undoubted physical presence—she is already a beautiful, well-developed young woman—and the

Dragon's invincible self-belief. There are already signs of Lady Helen throwing her ample weight around, resulting in her nickname, 'The Royal Raver'. This might not be far from the mark, although another, 'Melons' is perhaps a bit over the top, even for a busty Dragon. The fact that Lady Helen ended her spell at Gordonstoun with only one A level (art) is neither here nor there. Dragons don't get to lead the parade by passing exams but by being noticed. They demand to be accepted for what they are, not what they *might* be.

A Dog, Lord Nicholas will be a loyal son and devoted to his Tiger brother. But relationships take a dip with the Dragon sister. There is little understanding between social reformer and carnival leader in spite of the love so frequently offered and taken on both sides. Nicholas's future will be, in every sense, dogged by having Lady Helen as his closest sibling. However, there is always the Pig father's understanding to hand, one which will do much to calm the Dog's tendency to become anxious.

12
The Duke and Duchess of Gloucester

The Duke of Gloucester
Birthdate: 26 August 1944
Born in the Year of the Monkey

The Duchess of Gloucester
Birthdate: 20 June 1946
Born in the Year of the Dog

A pronounced characteristic of the Monkey personality is to be found in their ability to adapt. No other animal sign has the same facile ease to abandon a project when it goes badly and take up something else, often in a quite different field. In the case of Richard, Duke of Gloucester, the decision to alter his life was not one of his own making. It came about when his brother Snake William died suddenly in an air crash. Overnight Richard was faced with taking on his brother's title and the responsibilities of running the 2,500 acre family estate. Richard adapted without so much as a blink. In one decisive move he abandoned his north London architectural practice and headed for Northamptonshire to run his family's farms and estate.

The job of architect is one well suited to the complex mind of the Monkey. Britain's most celebrated architect, Sir Christopher

Wren, was a Monkey, and so was Leonardo da Vinci. Monkeys love to unravel knots and solve problems; their agile minds forever seeking new challenges. In common with so many Monkeys, Richard, Duke of Gloucester, also enjoys spreading his interests over a wide field. Monkeys hate to be put in boxes or categorized, which is perhaps why Richard is the principal patron of such a diverse number of organizations. Numbering over 50, they include: the Society of Engineers, the Institute of Advanced Motorists, the Pestalozzi Children's Village Trust, and the Homeopathic Research Foundation.

Another way the Monkey's keenness for new experiences expresses itself is through travel. Most Monkeys can't resist the opportunity of a trip to far-flung places and Richard has represented the Queen in countries ranging from China and Dubai to Kenya and the Solomon Islands. In fact, Richard spent his childhood in Australia, where his father was Governor-General. And there is another way Richard's particular animal sign makes its presence felt. The Chinese say Monkeys adore sweet things and are not usually abstemious. Although Richard neither smokes or drinks (he is the titular head of ASH—Action for Smoking and Health) he does love chocolate. Incidentally, it is believed the only way to lure Monkeys into a trap is by offering them something sweet.

The Chinese Horoscopes say that Monkeys waste no time making up their minds. On his second day at Cambridge, Richard met Birgitte Van Deurs, a Danish language student. He fell in love at once and they married in 1972, the Year of the Rat, which is a five-star special for Monkeys. Although Monkeys and Dogs get a zero mark when in love, the pairing mysteriously earns three out of five stars for marriage. This has, perhaps, something to do with the Monkey coming into daily contact with Dog's idealism and finding it has a positive influence on their own variable moral horizons.

Whereas some Dogs are over-fed and spoilt, becoming a pain in the neck for all but their most loyal friends, the majority are true to their sign of idealism. The Duchess of Gloucester is clearly the latter, a typically domestic Dog who puts her family first and is not over-anxious about life's many insoluble problems. There is not a breath of scandal about the Duchess of Gloucester and for most of us she remains a well-balanced Dog, who is universally well liked and who carries out her domestic duties with an enviable earnestness.

Richard's mother, Princess Alice, was born on Christmas Day 1901. As one might expect from a Buffalo, Princess Alice has played an important role in creating a solid foundation for the present Gloucester family. Her firm and dedicated personality has made her one of the royal favourites. During the war she was heavily involved with the Red Cross, the Women's Royal Voluntary Service, and the St John's Ambulance Brigade. Luckily for Richard, a Buffalo mother is expected to have a productive relationship with a Monkey son, which seems to have been the case.

The children

Parenthood is a strong feature of Monkey people, who take the job of bringing up their young very seriously. The Gloucesters' three children are: Alexander, a Tiger (born 24 October 1974), Davina, a Snake (born 19 November 1977), and Rose, a Monkey (born 1 March 1980). As siblings, their animal signs do not have a great deal of understanding—the Tiger and Snake having absolutely nothing in common. But the Monkey father and Monkey daughter score maximum-plus for compatibility. And there are three stars each for Monkey father with Tiger son and Snake daughter. Dog mum and Tiger son again get a top star rating, but the daughters achieve only one star for a Monkey and zero for a Snake.

As for the three children's futures, their signs would suggest that the Tiger, Alexander (Earl of Ulster), will attract the most attention in the early stages. Whatever his parents decide, if it is against his wishes, he will not conform. Alexander will choose his own destiny and fight tooth and claw to secure it. Rose will be vain and attention-seeking, as with most female Monkeys, and she might well turn her adaptable young hand to her father's old profession—architecture. In the case of the Snake daughter, Lady Davina, anything is possible. Not helped by the fact that Snakes take a painfully long time to mature, they only really make their mark in the peaceful worlds of art and religion. Snakes also tend to hang around doing nothing until they get the call from within. Something in the arts, interior design perhaps, is what Davina will end up doing before she bewitches the man of her choice.

13
Princess Alexandra and The Hon. Angus Ogilvy

Princess Alexandra
Birthdate: 25 December 1936
Born in the Year of the Rat

The Hon. Angus Ogilvy
Birthdate: 14 September 1928
Born in the Year of the Dragon

At last, a royal pairing with 100 per cent compatibility in all departments! Dragons and Rats are a perfect match and given that there are at least a dozen five-star relationships it is extraordinary, to say the least, that only one set of major royals managed to get it right. Admittedly, Prince Charles, as a future King, found his choice of partners limited, but we are left shaking our heads at how spectacularly wrong his choice was—at least according to the Chinese Horoscopes. Alexandra and Angus were, of course, under nothing like the pressure from the Queen to marry the 'right' person, nor were they victims of the same intense public scrutiny. The result was that their natural instincts were given a greater degree of exercise and, as a consequence, Princess Alexandra and Angus Ogilvy continue to provide an ideal picture of the Dragon and Rat in tandem. The Rat and

Dragon enjoy a rich mixture of emotional, intellectual and physical bonds which has few equals in the world of animal signs. Both Angus and Alexandra adore riding, playing tennis, and going to the theatre—all of which underline their signs' enjoyment in things both physical and spiritual. It is, however, music that gives the Ogilvys the greatest mutual pleasure, which is hardly surprising when we remember how many Rats and Dragons have been great composers and musicians. From Mozart to Irving Berlin (Rats), from Yehudi Menuhin to Placido Domingo (Dragons)—the list is endless.

In my mixed career I have met most of the Royal Family, and I can say without hesitation that Princess Alexandra is the most beautiful of women. She is everyone's image of an ideal princess and it does not surprise me that of all the present crop of princesses it is she who inspires nothing but wholehearted admiration. Apart from her naturally lovely skin and hair, she has a regal stature which is totally devoid of bogus pomp, and eyes that quite literally sparkle with excitement and curiosity. Charm, the Rat's sign, pours from her like water from a spring and her quick smile leaves one in no doubt as to her keen sense of humour. I met her at a charity dinner at the Savoy Hotel. My jazz band had been playing, along with a rag-bag of entertainers giving their services free, and after the show Princess Alexandra came backstage to meet the artists. Such is the broad and genuine scope of her interests that the Princess spoke to everyone, from a rather tacky drag-queen act (which she found fascinating) to the very large group of Hari Krishna singers.

Angus Ogilvy is a typical Dragon, and he would have to be in order to make the partnership with his charming Rat wife so auspicious. The Dragon's sign is luck and Angus was certainly lucky to have found his tutor at Oxford such a big help. Angus studied modern greats at Trinity (economics, history and philosophy), his economics tutor being the late Labour intellectual Anthony Crosland, born in the year of the Horse. It was Crosland, with his Horse sense and practical attitudes who more than anyone helped develop Angus's emerging business skills and set him on the path to an outstanding success in the extremely competitive world of high finance. But for all the Dragon's luck, it must be said that many are prone to view big business as a kind of cage, a state which represents a permanent threat to the freedom-loving Dragon personality.

As might be expected, Angus and the City did not last and in the 1960s he was connected with Lonrho, a company which had close links with Ian Smith's UDI party at the time of sanctions against Southern Rhodesia. Angus Ogilvy was forced to resign his directorship and thereafter concentrated his energies more on the needy and more soul-enhancing world of charity fund raising. Dragons are as renowned for their short tempers as Roosters are for their frankness, and Angus's part in the Lonrho affair elicited a classic Dragon response in a discussion with the Rooster Duke of Edinburgh. 'You've landed us in it this time,' the Duke barked. The response was immediate, 'Well,' Angus replied, 'at least I don't have a sister-in-law who's shacking up with a hippy'.

Angus Ogilvy has provided dozens of examples that illustrate his Dragon sign's influence—the need to be self-reliant being a constant factor. For example, Angus refused the Queen's offer of a grace and favour residence in Kensington Palace, opting for a £200,000 mortgage to buy their current home in Richmond Park. The Queen also offered him an Earldom which he refused with the same lack of diplomacy that all Dragons seem dogged by. He said simply, 'I don't see why I should get a peerage just because I married a princess'.

The children

The Ogilvys' children help make up an extremely auspicious family. James, born on 29 February 1964 is the same sign as his father, making a total of no fewer than six Dragons in the immediate Royal Family. Marina is a Fire Horse, born on 31 July 1966. Both Dragons and Horses share much in common, although it must be said that a Rat mother sometimes finds the independent and occasionally vain Horse a little tough to take. But there is nothing but admiration from the Dragon father for the Horse daughter, although he might just occasionally find himself and the Dragon son short-fused at the same time.

As to the question of Marina's and James's futures, the only truly safe answer is to say that in both cases it remains unpredictable. With Dragons and Horses, freedom is a paramount need with large helpings of luck also playing a dominant rôle. And it might be added that the Fire Horse daughter is the only discord in an otherwise perfectly tuned family. The Chinese Horoscopes point out that there is a problem facing Fire Horses, especially daughters. It is thought they experience everything life offers in extremes. Good and bad luck comes in equally massive doses and continues to do so through a Fire Horse's eventful life. As a result, Marina will certainly make some kind of name for herself, possibly using the Horse's practical skills. But whatever she chooses, her life will never be easy. James, on the other hand, will probably find things a touch too soft. As with his Dragon cousins, Prince Edward, Lady Helen Windsor, and Lady Sarah Armstrong-Jones, James Ogilvy will doubtless live a charmed life, one in which he will establish his own very clear-cut identity. Having read for an arts degree, the chances are he'll use this as a vehicle to express his Dragon sign's need for emotional freedom and enter the creative world.

In July of the Dragon year 1988, James married a fellow Dragon, Julia Rawlinson. Plenty of fireworks at the beginning for two Dragons, but to have married in a Dragon year may help the couple to go the distance.

14
Queen Victoria and Prince Albert

Queen Victoria
Birthdate: 25 April 1819
Born in the Year of the Cat

Prince Albert
Birthdate: 26 August 1819
Born in the Year of the Cat

Given the options, it is a curious fact that we must go back to the last century to find a monarch who married a wholly compatible partner as determined by the Chinese Horoscopes. Both Victoria and Albert were born under the sign of the Cat, which earns five stars in every department. A pair of Cats have complete understanding in love, marriage, and business. Given such compatibility it is little wonder that at one time Albert even acted as his wife's private secretary. A marriage between two Cats is almost certain to place a heavy emphasis on the home and they will form a profound attachment to what they put in them. Cats are nothing if not acquisitive and have a keen nose for what is beautifully made and fashionable. When they furnish a room, they do so to provide comfort and pleasure in equal measure. Paintings, carpets, works of art, all are carefully considered under the Cat's refined influence. Quick to spot trends, Cats quickly step into line. Victoria was the first-ever monarch to be filmed and to use electric lights and a telephone.

Albert and Victoria could be said to have spent their entire lives together building fabulous homes, which were filled to overflowing with tasteful and expensive objects and works of art. Indeed, so finely tuned was their collective taste that Albert and Victoria spawned a look which has survived intact to the present day. For almost three-quarters of a century, it is said, the sun never set on Victoria's empire, and the style of everything, from doorknobs to public buildings, bore her name—and the Cat's influence.

The Chinese say that Cats always prefer the hearth to the Big Wide World, and although Victoria and her consort presided over territories in every corner of the globe, they were clearly both happiest at home. Victoria painted extremely well, mainly small but effective watercolours, while her husband Albert displayed no little talent in the field of architecture. He was, after all, chiefly responsible for the Great International Exhibition of 1851. Cats also enjoy large familes—given the choice—and family life is essential to the well-being of all feline couples. Albert and Victoria had nine children and it is quite possible they would have produced more if Albert had not have died in 1861, aged only 42.

The Chinese emphasize that Cats, as virtuous, warm, and sensuous as they may well be, do not react well to sudden reversals. Too much pressure and you will find the Cat caving in. When faced with grief, Victoria found it all-consuming. Following Albert's untimely death, she locked herself away from public life, living in all but total seclusion for the best part of 20 years. Victoria never fully recovered from her husband's death, the monuments and museums that she built to his memory only adding to her sense of loss. The words she wrote in her journal shortly after Albert's death are typical of a Cat whose world has been torn apart: 'My <u>life</u> as a <u>happy</u> one is <u>ended</u>! The world is gone for <u>me</u>.' The underlining is the Queen's and adds a pathetic stress to the spare, almost childish sentiment. Again, the Chinese point out that Cat ladies are prone to tears and cry easily.

Placing the tears to one side, Cats are deeply sensuous and Victoria was no exception. A dozen or so examples exist which illustrate her highly sexual nature, and her physical relationship with Albert. She recorded that he put her stockings on for her and she kept a painting of a nude goddess, a gift from Albert, locked in a private drawer. On their honeymoon, Victoria wrote of 'Albert's excessive love', and how 'We kissed each other again and again'. When told that she could have no more children, Victoria asked, 'Oh, doctor, can I have no more fun in bed?'

In addition to the many classic Cat traits she inherited, Queen Victoria added longevity. Cats are thought to have nine lives, which in China is translated as long life. She died at 6:30 on the evening of 22 January 1901, aged 82. Queen Victoria had reigned for 64 years, 39 of which had been spent, as she put it herself 'On a dreary, sad pinnacle of solitary grandeur'.

15
Queen Elizabeth I

Queen Elizabeth I
Birthdate: 7 September 1533
Born in the Year of the Snake

Whereas in many other countries there have been any number of monarchs, potentates, sovereigns, shoguns, emperors and caliphs born in the Year of the Snake, we in Britain must go back nearly 300 years to find a Snake residing on the seat of power. If America and India have seen the likes of John F. Kennedy, Abraham Lincoln, Mahatma Gandhi and Indira Gandhi, all Snakes who enjoyed influential periods in office, England has only enjoyed the Snake's subtle and wise leadership on two occasions: Elizabeth I and Queen Anne. Both Snake queens illustrated perfectly the most positive aspects of their animal sign, but because of Elizabeth's longer reign (45 years as opposed to Anne's 12) her influence is the more clearly identifiable. The very term, Elizabethan rightly evokes an age which remains unmatched for its artistic scope and richness.

All historians agree that Elizabeth I was a woman capable of an almost bewitching charm. Men who met her fell under her spell and, as expected from female Snakes, Elizabeth used her innate powers to their full advantage. One bewitched victim was Christopher Hatton, a member of the Queen's bodyguard. The hapless

Hatton wrote to Elizabeth, 'To serve you is heaven, but to lack you is more than hell's torment'. Heady language from a commoner to the Queen. But Elizabeth met her romantic match in Robert, Earl of Leicester. Although married, it is believed that he was the only man Elizabeth truly loved, which would underline an important feature of the Snake sign. The Chinese say that Dragons love Snakes, and once they reciprocate a Snake will never let go of their emotional involvement. No prizes for guessing that Robert was born on 15 June 1532, the year of the Dragon.

Elizabeth also fell for a Tiger, the Earl of Essex, born on 10 October 1566. Clearly this was a love formed from the attraction of opposites. Snakes and Tigers get zero marks for understanding, which perhaps explains why Elizabeth eventually had the ambitious Earl beheaded. Mary Queen of Scots was another figure who featured heavily in Elizabeth's life, a beautiful and powerful woman who also ended up with her head on the block. Like Essex, Mary was Tiger, born on 8 December 1542.

Snakes are poor decision makers when pushed, but left to take their time their counsel is extremely wise, as befits their sign— they are born under the sign of wisdom. Snakes are artistic to an almost unparalleled degree, being appreciative of painting and the theatre, and exceptionally fond of music. During her reign the arts flourished as never before or, in the eyes of many, since. Elizabeth was herself a gifted player of the virginals and wrote poetry. Religious by inclination, many Snake ladies write with insight and strong imagery. The following poem survives to more than highlight Elizabeth's Snake influence:

> Christ was the Word that spake it,
> He took the bread and break it,
> And what the Word doth make it,
> I do believe and take it.

The Chinese point out that a curious feature of Snake women is a love of accessories. Elizabeth adored them. Self-centred and vain in sometimes painfully obvious ways, female Snakes would rather die than be seen looking drab. When Elizabeth's hair grew thin she wore a ridiculous red wig encrusted with gems. She whitened her skin with a mixture of powdered egg shells, lead, and alum, and her wardrobe included over 2,000 fabulous dresses. There is even a story which tells how she had a finger amputated as a result of refusing to remove a favourite ring which had grown too tight, a strong indication of the Snake's possessiveness. Elizabeth's accessories were used to their full advantage. In an age bubbling with intrigue, plot and counter-plot, a monarch quite literally had to have their head placed firmly on their shoulders. Elizabeth instinctively knew how to manipulate men. She played on their vanities and pandered to their ambitions. Her last words were typical of the wise Snake who has seen too late that truth is to be found outside wealth, power and influence. "All my possessions,' she begged, 'for one moment of time.'

16
King Henry VIII

King Henry VIII
Birthdate: 28 June 1491
Born in the Year of the Pig

F ew kings of England can be said to fit their animal sign as perfectly as Henry VIII—a porker from his head to his tail. Pigs work hard and play even harder. Social and fun-loving, Pigs burn the candle at both ends, as Henry displayed at one of the biggest parties ever thrown. Known today as 'The Field of the Cloth of Gold', this massive bun fight was held near Calais, lasted three weeks and had a guest list of over 5,000. The event was a Pig's delight, complete with singing, dancing and jousting, and involved the slaughter of more than 2,500 luckless animals. No-one counted the number of bottles of wine.

No other animal enjoys dressing up with such relish or does so with such effect. A peek at Henry's vast wardrobe would have revealed the very latest satins, velvets, silks, taffetas, plumes, jewels, and golden ornaments. And he wore them beautifully, paying enormous attention to detail. As a young man he was considered extremely handsome, an image helped no doubt by his classy line in clothes. Normally, Pigs are robust and quick to learn, although they sometimes have an over-exaggerated opinion of their often quite considerable intelligence. Henry could speak several languages, compose music, paint, and write poetry. He nevertheless lacked genuine insight into both people and the world at large, which the Chinese Horoscopes point out is a common fault in those born in the Year of the Pig.

The Chinese say Pigs tend to put their argument too forcefully in the initial stages of a discussion and are frequently obliged to back down. More to the point in the case of Henry VIII, it is also said that Pigs are easily duped and, lacking initiative, only work at their best when in partnership. Henry VIII was no exception and, his marriages to one side for the moment, throughout his life the King turned to others for advice and help. Three men played an important part in Henry's reign—Thomas Wolsey, Thomas Cranmer and Thomas Cromwell. Cranmer was a Rooster—not the best of partners for a Pig—while both Cromwell and Wolsey were Snakes. The open-hearted Pig is easily seduced by the Snake's subtle thinking, as Henry proved by allowing himself to be deeply influenced by both Cromwell and Wolsey.

Since Snakes of both sexes are capable of exercising great power over the Pig, it is not surprising to discover they also featured heavily in Henry's marital life. No less than three of his six wives were born in a Snake year—Katherine of Aragon, Jane Seymour, and Catherine Howard. But Pigs are dangerous when crossed. Their normally easy-going self-assurance turns inward, forcing the Pig to become ruthless in the extreme. And because they are so easily led by others, whose advice might not always be in the Pig's best interest, there is no limit to the damage a Pig in an angry frame of mind might inflict. We have only to recall Pig Ronald Reagan's bombing of Libya to get the point.

Three of Henry's wives came to an untimely end as a result of his Pig's influence turning sour. Catherine Parr was a Monkey and, as is typical of her sign, cleverly out-witted her then old and feeble Pig King. Katherine of Aragon died of a broken heart and Jane Seymour died in childbirth. But not so Catherine Howard, who lost her head for adultery. Having freed himself from the Snake's clutches Henry married Anne of Cleeves, a Pig two generations younger than her King. A pair of Pigs usually expect a five-star relationship, although they might easily end up trying to out-dress and out-play each other. In many cases, when animals of the same sign mirror their most negative sides, the relationship has little hope of surviving, no matter how high the score for compatibility. Having married three Snakes and a Pig, Henry tried a Cat. Anne Boleyn was a Cat, a sign which would normally enjoy a close relationship with a Pig. But records show she talked too much, probably acted a little too vainly, upstaging her pompous husband at the wrong moment, and, unhappily, followed Anne and Catherine to the block.

17
England's Kings and Queens

Rats

George I, Charles I, Mary I, Stephen, Count of Blois

Born under the sign of charm, Rats are reckless opportunists who use their considerable wits to their full advantage. Charles I was a classic Rat. Forever overdrawn, Charles spent like the King he was and as well as imposing swingeing taxes he even stooped to trying to sell off the Crown Jewels during a particularly sticky financial patch. At the same time his good taste produced a collection of royal art unequalled to this day. George I was no less of a Rat, even if he didn't speak English. Hating England, he spent most of his life in Germany enjoying huge meals and a string of mistresses paid for by the British taxpayer. As for Mary Tudor, it must be emphasized that all Rats experience an undercurrent of aggression. Bloody Mary gave into this trait by murdering a large number of subjects for being members of the wrong religion.

Buffaloes

George V, Edward VII, Henry VII, Henry VI, Richard I, Henry II, Edward III

Of all the Buffalo Kings, George V stands out as being one of the most typical. Firmly conservative in all walks of life his hobbies were stamp collecting and the sea. His main concern was that all the palace clocks should be exactly right and his interest in the world outside is perhaps best summed up by his description of German: 'A rotten language which I find very difficult'. But he cared passionately for all things British and his last words were, 'How is the Empire?' Buffaloes are also known for their prowess in battle (Napoleon, Hitler, etc.). Complex at heart, Richard I, also known as Richard Coeur de Lion, was no slouch when it came to wielding the broadsword, as a number of Jews and Arabs unhappily discovered. Buffaloes are deep creatures and fond of institutions, which many of them set up. Not surprisingly a Buffalo, Henry VI, founded Eton. Buffaloes are born under the twin signs of tenacity and endurance, and love hard work, which is perhaps why on his death bed, Edward VII said, 'No, I shall not give in. I shall go on. I shall work to the end.'

Tigers

Elizabeth II, William III, Mary II, James I, Edward V

In China you will never find two Tigers marrying. The relationship gets minus stars for compatibility, which is perhaps the reason why when Mary heard she was to marry William she wept for two whole days. Born under the sign of courage, Tigers act impulsively. This trait was illustrated by James I who suddenly knighted a loin of beef, thus giving butchers the label 'sirloin of beef' to hang in their shops. The Chinese say that Tigers born in the daytime face a life of danger and sudden death. No records exist of Edward V's hour of birth, but he certainly died sudden-ly—suffocated in the Tower, aged 13.

Cats

Victoria, Henry III, Henry V

There is no doubting the extent to which Cats will go to acquire beautiful things. Born under the sign of virtue, Cat people of both sexes adore refinement and will spent much of their time sur-rounding themselves with wonderful objects. This was certainly true of Henry III, who built the finest religious building in Britain—Westminster Abbey, described as a monument to his artistic taste. And, like all Cats, he put his family first. Such was his favouritism towards his wife and her family it caused the Baron's War. Cats are excellent diplomats and administrators, which is almost certainly why Henry V enjoys such an outstanding reputation for having been both.

Dragons

William I

The only Dragon king—how different from China where practi-cally every single leader is a Dragon—William I is nevertheless a first-class representative of his sign. Dates differ as to his precise year of birth and although William was responsible for the Domesday Book, which would be more in keeping with the methodical Cat (suggesting he was born in 1027), William the Conqueror was thought to be one of the luckiest kings of all time. Every scholar says as much. Since Dragons are born under the sign of luck I won't argue. Another strong clue is that fact that the Chinese say that Dragons are prone to overeating. At his death William was so fat he burst open in his coffin, filling the church with a foul smell.

Snakes

Anne, Elizabeth I

Snakes are the most sexually orientated of all the 12 signs, and this is no doubt the reason why Queen Anne was pregnant 18 times. Snake ladies are not usually heavy drinkers but I imagine that in Anne's case it was largely to dull her violent and often sexually confused inner passions. As well as having 17 children—one baby died prematurely—Anne had a terrible crush on Sarah Churchill, to whom she wrote reams of love letters. In keeping with Snakes everywhere, Anne was very religious (in spite of the gin).

Horses

Edward VIII, George IV, George III, Charles II, Henry IV, Canute

Horses are practical folk and the Chinese say that they have a marked degree of success in political matters, usually leading through a powerful personality. Charles II could not have been more like a Horse. The Merry Monarch was hugely popular and had bags of humour and wit—two very Horsey traits. He was also weak in love, another sign of the Horse's influence, enjoying a string of mistresses that included the delightful Nell Gwynne. A mixture of the influence of his Horse's practical nature and open heart were perhaps best expressed in Charles's famous last words: 'Don't let poor Nelly starve'. Mistresses also featured heavily in the life of George IV, the only English monarch to commit bigamy. Horses are believed to be vain creatures, doubtless the reason why the Prince Regent, a man of style and elegance, and once called an 'Adonis of loveliness' during his decline, stooped to greeting his public in cosmetics and stays. Practicality is a pronounced feature of the Horse and a hallmark of King Canute's reign. The story of him trying to turn back the tide was not to prove that he was invincible—quite the opposite. Canute sat in the sea to show his sycophantic followers just how human he really was.

Goats

George VI, Richard II

Goats are born under the sign of art and Richard II, as well as inventing the handkerchief, made his court a sparkling centre for the arts and culture. However, the Chinese point out that Goats have a deeply capricious nature, especially in sexual matters. Richard was no exception. As well as coping with being gay in a somewhat butch world, he had problems with his second wife. A girl 23 years his junior, Isabella of France was only seven years old when Richard proposed; no prying social workers in those days! Richard also leaned heavily on John of Gaunt, who tethered the young Goat and helped him produce his best. Gaunt was a Dragon, and there are those who say he actually ran the show, a fact which would not surprise anyone familiar with the Chinese Horoscopes.

Monkeys

Richard III, Henry I, Harold II

Although the commonly accepted view of Richard III is through pro-Tudor eyes, i.e. Shakespeare's, there can be no argument that Richard Crouchback was a pretty devious fellow. Monkeys love intrigue, to trick and plot, and there can have been few more devious, tricky, plot-laying kings than Richard. He murdered most of his family and just about anyone else who upset his carefully laid schemes. If his last words were, 'A horse, a horse, my kingdom for a horse', it would only underline the Monkey's insatiable appetite for wheeling and dealing. He would no doubt have offered his grandmother into the bargain, if he had one. On the credit side, Monkeys are great administrators, as Henry I proved (so was Richard, by the way). The Monkey also has a great thirst for knowledge and learns extremely quickly. This was certainly the case of Henry who, after his death, was dubbed 'Beauclerc', or the Scholar in recognition of his outstanding learning.

Roosters

William IV, James II, Edward VI, Edward IV, Lady Jane Grey, William II

Of all the Kings and Queens, those born in a Rooster year seem to fit their influence more perfectly than any other. Each is distinguished by at least one pronounced characteristic. Take William IV, for example, perhaps the most typical royal Rooster of all. Roosters are born under the sign of candour and William IV's remarks were so outspoken that his ministers were often deeply embarrassed. When shown a fine old master purchased by his brother, George IV, William remarked openly, 'My brother was very fond of this Knicknackery. Damned expensive taste, though.' And when King Leopold of the Belgians asked for a glass of water, William's instant response was, 'God damn it, why don't you drink wine?' Roosters do not like to be forced into action, preferring always to go at their own pace. Lady Jane Grey illustrated this point with classic Rooster style when she was suddenly told to be Queen. Most people would jump at the chance; Lady Jane flatly refused. The Chinese say that Roosters love to write things down on bits of paper or into books, diaries and so on. This might be one of the reasons Edward IV supported William Caxton to set up the first printing press in England. And I've always thought it fitting, given that Roosters have red crowns, that William II should be known as William Rufus, because of his red hair.

Dogs

It is curious that a nation so full of the bulldog breed has never had a Dog as monarch. This will change when young Prince William succeeds to the throne. In the meantime we will just have to content ourselves with the fact that Winston Churchill, the most famous of all British Dogs was as strong as any King. The day William is crowned will be a great day for Britain. Much cheering and barking I expect.

Pigs

John, George II, Oliver Cromwell (Lord Protector), Henry VIII, Edward I

There are a number of animal signs who function better when in a partnership. Pigs are such animals. It should be added that when given supreme power the normally robust and honest porker often gets delusions of grandeur, causing him to behave in a totally opposite manner. Honesty turns to treachery, generosity becomes meanness and the lovable peace-lover is replaced by a mean-minded war-monger. John was a classic example of a Pig king who could have done with a little more throne sharing to expose his better side. His despotic rule got so out of hand that John was forced to sign the Magna Carta, thus handing over power to the people. George II was a more conventional Pig in the Chinese sense. He was robust, well informed and keen on the minutiae of court etiquette. He was also helped by a genuine love of his wife, Queen Caroline. With a touching hint of the Pig's open heart, when Caroline died following a long illness, George said sadly, 'I never saw one fit to buckle her shoe'. I have yet to decide if his own death was typical of the Pig—he died of a heart attack while sitting on the loo. I can find no reference to this anywhere in the Chinese Horoscopes.

Select Bibliography

Nicholas Bentley, *Golden Sovereigns* (Mitchell Beazley, 1970).

Stephen Birmingham, *Duchess* (Futura, 1981).

Michael Block (ed.), *Wallis and Edward* (Weidenfeld & Nicolson, 1986).

Craig Brown and Lesley Cunliffe, *The Book of Royal Lists* (Routledge & Kegan Paul, 1982).

Nigel Dempster, *HRH The Princess Margaret* (Quartet Books, 1981).

Donald Edgar, *Prince Andrew* (Arthur Barker, 1980).

Antonia Fraser (ed.), *The Lives of the Kings and Queens of England* (Weidenfeld & Nicolson, 1975).

Alan Hamilton, *The Royal Handbook* (Mitchell Beazley, 1985).

Anthony Holden, *Charles Prince of Wales* (Weidenfeld & Nicolson, 1979).

G. L. Hough, *Chambers Dictionary of Dates* (Chambers, 1983).

Robert Lacey, *Majesty* (Hutchinson, 1977).

John Pearson, *The Ultimate Family* (Michael Joseph, 1986).

Tim Satchell, *Royal Romance* (Penguin, 1986).

Christopher Warwick, *Princess Margaret* (Weidenfeld & Nicolson, 1983).

Audrey Whiting, *The Kents* (Hutchinson, 1985).

E. N. Williams, *Dictionary of English and European History* (Penguin, 1980).

Rosemary York (compiler), *Charles in His Own Words* (Omnibus Press, 1981).